1.8 MILLION MINUTES AND COUNTING

CELEBRATING & CONTEMPLATING MY FIRST 40 YEARS IN JEWISH BROADCASTING

BY NACHUM SEGAL
WITH YAFA STORCH

© All rights reserved
First Edition 2024

For any questions or comments:
yigal@nachumsegal.com

For Staci,

Mersh Was Right.

I Hit The Jackpot!

TABLE OF CONTENTS

Acknowledgments vii
Introduction 1
History 7
Family 23
Jewish Music 37
Jewish Heroes 49
Partnerships 61
Zionism 69
You Don't Have to be Jewish 87
Jewish Radio Phenomenon 95
Promoting Causes 111
Political Involvement 125
Positive Programming 137
Shlomo Carlebach 149
Jewish Unity Initiative 157
Top Ten 165
How Would You Like Your Show? 175
JM in the AM Traditions 191
Fire 203
Epilogue - Israel at War 209
Glossary 217

ACKNOWLEDGMENTS

Things have a way of working out well. With the wind of passion for radio at my back and the guidance of G-d in front of me, I had the good fortune to be at the right place at the right time. Forty years later, I can confidently and proudly complete this work while enjoying the accomplishments of the past four decades.

The book that you are holding came to fruition after a long process that tested the patience and fortitude of my co-author, Yafa Storch. Yafa's ability to create chapter after chapter of so many facets of my career was the key to bringing my whole story together as a complete book. Much of this work was completed years ago. Back then was not the right time for its release. All these years later, when I proposed picking up this project again, I was not sure how she would react. Yafa handled the entire years-long ordeal with great professionalism and enthusiasm and for that I am very grateful.

Thank you to Shloimie "Sam" Ash (notthemusicstore@gmail.com) whose insight has always been appreciated and whose creativity and talent has had a profound effect on me and resulted in the title and cover of this book.

When we began this book, many years ago, I was lucky to have Chava Willig Levy a"h as my editor. Her editing skills were unmatched and she had a keen understanding of our voice and vision. Her creative insight had an immeasurable influence on this book. I am saddened by her passing before we could finish this project together.

Before I got to WFMU, I embarked on this broadcasting journey from WYUR at Yeshiva University. I worked with many great fellow collegiates in a club where only we knew the extent of its coolness. Folks like Hindy and Saul Guberman, Jordy Alter, Chaim T Konig, Robert Katz, Amy Greenzweig Gelbart, Sora Kosowsky Gross and many others. My mentor at WYUR who changed my life was the late Howie Bramson. Howie paid careful attention to my first WYUR show as I was hosting and, once it was over, assured me that the show, which I felt was a radio train wreck, was a great first time effort. I remember that encounter like it was yesterday. Howie was a true leader and great team manager. His encouragement was priceless. He left us way too early in life. I remember going with Robert to visit him days before his passing. It was one of those "thank you for my career" moments. I wish he was around to read this book. He would have enjoyed every page.

Larry Wachsman and the late Norman Laster were two key figures in the story that got me started at WFMU. Norman, representing Dr Rhoda Freeman of Upsala College, the home of WFMU until 1992, called YU thinking that maybe there was a student who could take over the Jewish programming at WFMU. The call was directed to another true mentor of mine, Larry Wachsman, then the Director of Student Activities (including WYUR), who knew I would give my right arm to be the WFMU morning man. The next day, Erev Rosh Hashanah, I was on the air after a brief training session with outgoing host and YU basketball legend David Kufeld.

My experience at YU was enhanced by many great Rabbis and educators including by my mentor and guide, Dr Jeffrey S. Gurock, who has been a wonderful advisor and source of common sense for me for 40 years.

Many WFMU personalities have had an influence on my radio career and I thank all of them for the mutual respect and for the sincere encouragement that I received there from 1983-2016. For the majority of the time from 1985 to the present, WFMU has been led by Ken Freedman. Ken has a great appreciation for good radio. His recognition of how important JM in the AM was to the Jewish world and the radio world set him apart from many leaders in the industry who allowed their personal views to interfere with great programming. Ken is a great friend and although we have very different backgrounds, our relationship grew year after year and show after show. Some have suggested that Ken will have a great eternal reward due to his commitment to our efforts and our community. I couldn't agree more.

WFMU radio is a hub of volunteerism with few paid staff members. Producing and hosting a daily show generally needs a large staff and a large financial commitment. The JM in the AM (Jewish Moments in the Morning) team that formed around me as time went on was, and continues to be, a true beacon of volunteerism. My staff members have never earned a penny and, at the same time, could not be more committed to JM in the AM and the Nachum Segal Network. They all became household names in the Jewish world and have endured a lifetime of protecting me at every opportunity. There is no sufficient thank you for any of them. Mattes Weingast, Mark Zomick, Mayer Fertig, Robert Katz, the late Meir Weingarten, Randi Wartelsky, Chief Engineer Zalman Kopel and Social Media Director Yoni Pollak have together been the majority of our on-air presenters and superb substitute hosts. In addition, they took upon themselves many other responsibilities that have contributed to our success over the years.

I have never been able to sufficiently express to Mattes and Mark the appreciation I have for their loyalty and commitment. I thank them for the endless hours of dedication to me and NSN through thick and thin. I don't deserve such devoted friends. G-D felt otherwise.

In addition to being a substitute host and an on air presenter, Miriam L Wallach served as General Manager of NSN for ten years and continues to represent me as my manager. Miriam and I worked to create and maintain a 24 hour media presence in the Jewish world and her innovative and creative ideas and projects helped escalate NSN to a premier level. We continue to take advantage of her insight and guidance to benefit our staff and listeners. Thank you Miriam for everything you have done to make me and NSN an even greater force in our global community.

Miriam's first mission was to attract many personalities who would enhance our daily presentation. She fulfilled that task brilliantly and, until today, we continue to benefit from the vast array of NSN program hosts that she recruited. I thank all of them for helping us reach more people in many different areas with more interesting and varied programming. It is an honor to have such a team.

Avrumi Finkelstein has been the backbone of NSN for over twenty years. Avrumi has never had a day off. He is the one in charge of supervising every technical aspect of our broadcasts. It continues to be a true delight to work with Avrumi and it is his dedication that keeps us running smoothly every day. I thank him for all the effort he puts into the network.

My Chief of Staff, Rabbi Yigal Segal, has worked with me for over twenty years and has been an incredible CFO, Business Manager and Director of Development. Leading all those departments is not easy. Yigal does it with love, enthusiasm and with a constant vision for the future. Working with a brother could be difficult. For me it has been the opposite. This book would never have come to fruition without his guidance, editing and encouragement and I cannot thank him enough.

It would be impossible to keep our operation going without generous sponsors and donors who understand the value of an inspirational media source that emphasizes Torah and Israel and who are proud to support it. Thank you to Bat Sheva and Murray Halpern, the extended Halpern family, Sindy Liben and family, Toby and Dr. Marc Singer, the Adelsberg family, Bea and Ralph Rosenbaum, the Herzog family of Royal Wine, The Rothenberg family, Sonia and Robert Gold A'H, Hon. Michael Bloomberg and the thousands of listeners, sponsors, donors, organizations and foundations that have been supporters for all or part of the past forty plus years.

It is important for me to publicly recognize two wonderful institutions that gave me opportunities that I always dreamed about and for which I am eternally grateful. I have been the High Holiday Cantor at The New Springville Jewish Center on Staten Island, NY from 1984 until today. It is an exhilarating experience to lead a congregation in its services on such prominent days. Thank you to Rabbi Segal, his wife, Babbi, their family and all the presidents, officers and congregants who have made it possible.

My thanks to Shlomo Brazil, Larry Stern and their associates. In 1989, they hired me as the founding head counselor of Camp Mesorah. It was the opportunity of a lifetime and was instrumental in shaping the person I have become. I take great pride in how the camp continues until today as a top choice in Jewish summer camps and additional pride that my son, Yehoshua, filled that HC role at Mesorah 35 years later.

I think back to the impact that my parents had on me and the influence of my siblings on my life (more about that in a later chapter).

Then I consider the values and commitment to our tradition that Staci and I have been able to pass on to the next generation, a generation that has begun to build its own families and has implemented its own missions to have a positive impact on Jewish life in the USA and in Israel. To Kayla and Binyamin, Chava, Lizzie and Yosef, Temimah and Yehoshua, Yonina and Eitan and Gavri, you and our grandchildren cannot make us any prouder. Mommy and I have sown seeds of leadership, commitment and passion, and you have blossomed into a garden of hope and principle, benefiting those around you and the Jewish people.

This book is dedicated to one person; Staci Segal. My late brother was right when he pointed out that I hit the jackpot when I married her. JM in the AM is my first love and Staci always knew that. She lives a life where she knows that my love for radio and my work was surpassed in 1989 by my love for her and the close connection and shared sense of purpose that we have felt from day one. The passionate nature of the radio industry and the tremendous attraction that the "theater of the mind" has always been is not easy for people outside of radio to understand. Staci has seen over the years and discovered early on the spirit, intensity and excitement that live radio has and how enjoyable my commitment to it continues to be. This book is a gift to her. I hope it slightly makes up for the lonely mornings, the unusual commitments and the sacrifice one must make when their spouse is a public figure. I thank her for the patience and flexibility for which she is known and which she utilizes with great positive purpose. The gift she has given me is our partnership which continues to build a wonderful family that makes so many so proud. We are grateful to G-d that we share each other's lives and I am grateful to her for being the foundation of mine.

INTRODUCTION

Marathon Friday 2007. It is hard to describe the mix of feelings I'm experiencing right now. Exhaustion? Yes. Nervousness? Definitely. But as we all await the last batch of pledges, hoping that the sleepless hours will have helped us meet — and perhaps even exceed — our financial goal, we sense that we're a part of something bigger than dollars and cents. Something that, as I take a minute to glance at the hub of activity surrounding me, I now realize has become a microcosm for what we do here all year round.

As these grueling two weeks of raising funds for the radio station approach completion, I'm surrounded by the usual cast. Mattes Weingast, my main co-host since 1984, is managing the phone room and the donations. Mark Zomick, my producer for decades, is prepping guests, fine-tuning our schedule and organizing the pledges. I don't know where I would be without them. And pacing back and forth, always ready to enhance the show from behind the scenes, is my old friend Joey Bodner. Helpful throughout the year — donating money, catering meals, or just lending a hand — he is particularly supportive, as are so many others, during Marathon Week.

Beside me at the mic, relieving my vocal cords for a few minutes by announcing more pledges, is Mayer Fertig. Each day over the last two weeks, another member of my loyal team has sat in that chair: Mayer Fertig, Robert Katz, Randi Wartelsky, and Meir Weingarten. Each in his/her own inimitable way has brought new character to the marathon — and to the show. This volunteer staff, offering both time and devotion so freely, is truly inspiring.

But what is equally amazing about our annual fundraising drive is the sight in front of me as I look through the glass separating the studio rooms, a sight that would be virtually unimaginable in any other Jewish venue. From near and far, spanning the spectrum of age, cultural identity and religious affiliation, people have congregated in our three-room studio to express their appreciation for what we do and to help ensure that it continues. They have dropped whatever they were doing to try, in their own way, to help this cause that they so strongly believe in. Radio's amazing capacity to unite has never been clearer.

Directly in front of me, I see an Orthodox man in a suit — he looks like he's on his way to work — who has taken an hour to answer phones. Next to him is an elderly woman who has been volunteering at the station for several years; she has told me that *JM in the AM* is her only connection to Judaism and that the least she can do is to help us out. In the far corner I can see a man recording pledges with the assistance of his two children; he has brought them along because he feels this is an important community service event for them to experience.

At the next table sits a group of tenth grade boys from TABC. They have come, with their principal, to be a part of Marathon Friday. Under normal circumstances, we do not allow anyone under the age of eighteen in the studio, but during the marathon we make an exception. Their youthful enthusiasm contributes a refreshing quality. At the same time, our studio is contributing something to them: a first-hand look at *Jewish Moments in the Morning*, a wholesome oasis in an otherwise exceedingly secular radio environment. They're having a great time, as did their peers from Kushner, JEC, Bruriah, Frisch, MTA and other schools earlier in the week.

I see many faces I've never seen before. It is truly gratifying that new people join our team each year. Equally gratifying is the fact that many volunteers return year after year. During our first marathon, back in 1984, a woman walked in with a box of Entenmann's donuts for us. She introduced herself as Hilda Strassman and explained that she was there to help in any way that she could. And indeed, she did just that — and more. Besides being the first "caterer" of the morning show, long before anyone else thought of nourishing our crew, Mrs. Strassman took pledges, inputted billing data, sent out entire mailings, and in fact, did anything and everything to be helpful. Because she never missed a day of the marathon, we got to know her and her husband, Buddy, very well. What's more, the listening audience became so familiar with her that we all mourned together when she suddenly passed away in 2000, at the age of 75.

Beyond the studio walls, the excitement of Marathon Week is still palpable. In addition to the pledges phoned in from all over the United States, we receive calls from around the world. "Have we reached our goal yet?" "Are we getting closer?" Our listeners really care. One year, a relative of mine was sitting in her car at 9:30 on the marathon's final morning, eagerly awaiting our final total. When the numbers were tallied and we announced that we had indeed reached our fundraising goal, she glanced out of her car window. To her left she saw a man in a yarmulke turn off his car radio, take the keys out of the ignition, and pump his fist in the air, exclaiming, "Yes!" Perhaps it was a victory felt throughout Klal Yisrael.

Year after year, I am amazed to discover that our show's audience keeps on growing. Yes, there are hints just about every week: an email from an Internet listener in South Africa, a call from a fan in Arizona. But the Marathon Week statistics are just astounding. With pledges from over 30 states — who would have guessed that there are Nebraskans who feel strongly about Jewish radio? — not to mention several countries overseas. How did I merit the privilege to be at the epicenter of this worldwide Jewish celebration?

Even more remarkable than the show's effect on geographical unity is its effect on cultural and religious unity. During this week alone, we have been honored with visits from the vice president of Agudas Yisrael, Rabbi Shlomo Gertzulin, as well as from local Jersey City residents who assert that *JM in the AM* is their only affiliation with Judaism. Prominent members of the Jewish music industry have stopped by to play their latest releases. Government officials from New York and New Jersey have come in to express their support. And last year, Marathon Friday featured a visit from New York City's Mayor Mike Bloomberg.

Looking back even further, I recall visits and pledges from hundreds of community leaders, rabbis, and principals, not to mention other representatives of Jewish organizational life. But since 2001, our biggest donor — by far — has been Barry Liben. Owner of one of the country's largest travel agencies, Tzell Travel, Barry originally called the station to ask us to announce the Beitar organization reunion he was helping to organize. We were happy to oblige and, as a result, he learned about the show, what we do, and what we represent. As his synagogue's past president, Barry is very committed to Jewish continuity, as is his family. Fascinated by our programming, he decided to make the show a beneficiary of his commitment to charity. Barry and his wife, Sindy, soon became our biggest contributors, donating $30,000 this year alone. Their generosity encouraged many others to increase their contributions.

Those large sums notwithstanding, with only a few hours to go on Marathon Friday, I am still nervous. Will we meet our fundraising goal?

My anxiety is rooted in the knowledge that radio is an industry based solely on habit. If you are in your car while the show is on, you'll tune in. But if your schedule changes, you no longer have the opportunity, or the motivation, to listen. With some significant exceptions, our list of donors changes considerably from year to year, and I never know who will end up giving. Thank G-d, we've always pulled through at the end, so I try to leave the worrying for the middle of the night. When I'm in the studio, I'm focused on the bigger picture: the excitement and the interaction we're generating.

I sometimes think of the marathon weeks and their holiday atmosphere as an association's annual convention, attended by people connected by a common interest, but who get to meet in person and strengthen their bonds only once a year. At other times, I see these weeks as a family reunion; if radio creates a family environment and does it well, then Jewish radio can create an even closer family — and does it better.

Of course, family members do not always agree. In fact, closeness and familiarity generate the most heated arguments. Who but your brother can tell you straight out when he thinks you're dead wrong about a choice you've made?

My extended family of listeners at *JM in the AM* and The Nachum Segal Network feels comfortable enough to express both admiration and annoyance. Listeners' letters in the earlier years, and then, emails, text messages, and app comments have been piling up at the studio and on our devices. Many have been answered, but, sadly, it is impossible for me to respond to them all.

That's why I have decided to compile some of the most thought-provoking, and compelling queries and comments, making them the springboard for the book you are holding in your hands. I have tried to address them to the best of my ability while giving you, I hope, a picture of what it is like to be on "the other side of the glass."

HISTORY

To: "Nachum Segal" <nachum@wfmu.org>
Subject: bad number

I live in Monroe (Kiryas Joel) and we happen to have the second fastest growing Jewish community in the world (next to Boro Park...).

Although listening to the radio is a hush matter in our community, I can personally tell you that every second person in town I know is a steady JM in the AM listener.

Furthermore, my younger brothers-in-law tell me that the management (hanhala) of their yeshiva is puzzled over the "morning hours mystery." The person who is hired to wake the boys in the morning (5:45) has almost no problem, as most of the boys are already up. But then, the shul remains empty till 9:00 a.m.! Little do they know that the boys are mostly hiding in the woodwork with their Walkmans, listening to Nachum Segal.

✻✻✻

Subject: W.Y.U.R. (Seeking Advice)
To: Nachum@wfmu.org

Dear Nachum,
I have recently taken over the prestigious position that you created. I am the Jewish music DJ at the YU radio station. I have been listening to your show for quite a long time, and I'm a huge fan. You happen to be my inspiration for trying out for the position and, thank G-d, getting it!

I was wondering if you could help me with several things. The radio station has no Jewish music collection. Funds are limited, as I'm sure you remember from your YU days. If you could please help me to connect with some of the distributors in terms of building up a CD library for the station, it would be great. If you have any other suggestions in terms of creating a CD library, it would also be very much appreciated. I am just starting out, so if you have any pointers for me, that would also be great. I hope to be able to ask you questions and look to you for advice in the future. I hope that, with your vast experience and success, you can help me mold my show into something great. Thank you very much for all your time and understanding.

Subject: Re: (no subject)
To: nachum@wfmu.org

Thanks, Nachum,

What is your "secret"?!? How do you manage to sound so "fresh" and "renewed" each morning and evening?

I guess you really love what you do.... We sure do love and look forward to your a.m. program each morning.

❋ ❋ ❋

To: Nachum@wfmu.org
Date: Wed, 6 Nov 2002 22:24:18 -0500
Subject: Mazel Tov

Dear Nachum AMV"S,
Mazel Tov on your new evening show. This past Monday there was much excitement at our home as we preset the remote so that 620 AM would be the first station on the AM channel for presets. Your signal comes in loud and clear.

Looking forward to hearing from you and seeing you.

❋ ❋ ❋

Subject: Hawaii hears you
To: nachum@jmintheam.org

You will soon have regular listeners in the US Army and Navy in Hawaii — and you know them!!!

At a beis avel last night in Morristown, I ran into visiting former Newarker, Shmuel Felzenberg. Remember him? Well, he is now THE Jewish Chaplain for all Jewish soldiers and sailors West of LA and east of Tokyo!

Based at an Army base in Oahu, he goes back home today to prepare for an amazing Menorah ceremony with the Governor of Hawaii — who, as you know, is Jewish.

Anyway, I gave Shmuel the hours of your show and he was thrilled to learn of the Archives, as you broadcast live to Hawaii from 1:00 AM -4:00 AM every morning — not exactly drive time.

It is hard to believe that I am old enough to write this chapter, old enough to reflect on a generation of service via the airwaves — in fact, to reflect on a generation of anything. People often ask how I got into the radio business, how it came about that one person could speak to so many Jews every day (to the greatest number of Jews, aside from the Prime Minister of Israel, my brother jokingly likes to point out.)

Alongside my own personal journey through the world of radio, the world itself has changed and evolved in so many significant ways. When I speak to children now, they can hardly relate to a world when the only way to reach such vast and varied segments of the Jewish community was to be featured on *JM in the AM*. For example, during the 1993 NYC mayoral election season, the two candidates, Giuliani and Dinkins, fought over access to our microphone, as they thought it was the best campaign method to procure the Jewish vote.

To address the changes around us, we have adapted, modifying our news segments to offer more analysis than reporting, and, as the audience grew to include listeners in all corners of the globe, we adjusted our announcements about local events. But, through it all we have maintained our emphasis on helping people; as the emails and app comments from fans indicate, we have continued to have a profound effect on our audience. In fact, as Covid hit in 2020, we received a large donation to the show with a note reading, "Continue what you are doing; we need you now more than ever."

When I look back at the sequence of events that has brought me to where I am today, I see clearly that lives are shaped by seemingly inconsequential episodes and that apparently random turns in the road can lead to thrilling developments. Each day brings new ideas, and the show, along with me, is still growing. Having reached the milestone of forty years in broadcasting, it seems appropriate to look back and ensure that we do not take for granted the amazing phenomenon we have been lucky to be a part of; nor the incredible people — relatives, mentors, colleagues, and friends — who have helped bring it to fruition.

I guess that, more than anyone, a mother always knows what her son really wants and needs. Because, to be perfectly honest, when I left for camp in the summer of 1981, I had never given serious consideration to a career in radio. True, I absolutely loved listening to that little box. I was totally enthralled by radio sportscasters, and, while I could rarely focus my attention on anything for more than a few minutes, radio could captivate me for hours on end. There are even clandestine tapes, saved by my sister, of me "broadcasting" sports reports when I was five and six years old. Still, it had never occurred to me that I could really do anything productive for our community with this obsession.

My mother knew better. As I boarded the bus for Camp Morasha the summer before my college career was to begin at YU, the last thing she said was, "While you're in camp, see if you can find out how to get a position at the YU radio station, I think it is something you'll enjoy." And so, I did. When I enrolled at YU that fall, I immediately applied for a show at WYUR. Despite my lack of experience, I was granted a program because I offered to do a Jewish music show while most applicants were looking to do mainstream music shows. Whatever the reason, I was more than happy to learn the ropes of radio broadcasting.

I tackled my first show with nervous anticipation, preparing a written script, practicing countless times, and even bringing my roommate along for assistance. Still, when the show ended at midnight, I was deeply disappointed in my performance; I had made significant technical errors and had flubbed my monologue. In retrospect, it is easy to see that radio is not a skill to be perfected in one evening. But that night, I was dejected, feeling that all my work had been for naught and that my love for radio was never going to get me anywhere.

Howie Bramson *a"h*, then WYUR's general manager, had stayed in the studio till midnight and stopped me on my way out. Immediately sensing my mood — I certainly did little to disguise my disappointment — he offered words of encouragement that I remember to this day. He was honest with me. I had made mistakes, but Howie thought it was a very good first show. He insisted that I displayed raw talent that needed to be honed. He suggested that I not listen to the show's recording that night, as it would only make me more upset. Instead, Howie advised me to review it slowly over the weekend and see what should be rectified.

I give Howie credit for starting me off on the right foot; without him, I would have most likely given up early in the game. Unfortunately, Howie contracted a fatal form of cancer several years later. When I visited him in the hospital, I thanked him profusely for all he had done and told him I would never have progressed without his help.

Broadcasting, like the board game Othello, takes "a minute to learn and a lifetime to master." I quickly caught on to the skills I needed and began the long and still evolving path to perfecting them. Unlike almost everything else in my life that bored me so quickly, radio captivated me. The more I became involved, the more I loved it. I would spend hours at the station, volunteering to substitute whenever I was needed, ready to give up anything else, regardless of its importance, when a broadcasting opportunity arose.

During the 1981 and 1982 season, the Thursday show that ran from 10:00 p.m. until midnight featured solely Jewish music; it was titled, *Simcha with Stretch*, a reference to my nickname and significant height. During the 1983 season, I began to include interviews with various Jewish personalities. In that same year, my commitment and dedication to the station, coupled with the rapport I had developed with the university's administration, earned me a promotion to general manager of WYUR. I was excited about the position, hardly expecting what would come next: perhaps the biggest turning point in my radio career.

HISTORY

WYUR Dinner 1982. Accepting award for The Simcha w/ Stretch Show from Sheldon Gladstein.

Two days before Rosh Hashana, I stopped by to say hello to Larry Wachsman, YU's head of student activities and with whom I had forged a relationship at Camp Morasha. He had just received a call from WFMU, the Upsala College radio station that for many years had featured a daily two-hour Jewish music show. The host was leaving and unless an immediate replacement was found, the show would fold. Larry asked if I'd be interested in filling the position, one that required my presence at the East Orange, New Jersey station at seven o'clock each weekday morning. I couldn't believe my luck. This was a golden opportunity, one that I never dreamed would come so soon. I instantly accepted the job.

I was walking on air. Bursting to inform my family, I headed over to my brother's office to tell him the news. From there, I called WFMU's outgoing host, David Kufeld, the YU basketball legend, who trained me the next day, Erev Rosh Hashanah. I began hosting the show that very same day.

*Rabbi Chaim Nate Segal, Rush Limbaugh & Nachum in Moshe Peking (NYC) 1988.
The night we met Rush.*

It was a thrilling time for me, getting my feet wet at a real radio station that reached thousands of listeners. The fact that the station reached as many people as it did in 1983 is an incredible story in itself. Being a college station, it should have been heard only on campus and slightly beyond. Due to an error in calculation, the coverage area was much greater than it should have been, an error that went undiscovered until 1989. This mistake brought the college extensive legal battles, as other local stations claimed WFMU encroached on their listening space.

The college countered that it was providing a unique service to the community by broadcasting freeform radio, a radio format in which the disc jockey is given total control over what music to play. It had to prove that contention, and it did so, in large part by underscoring the role that *JM in the AM* played. Indeed, the FCC ruled that WFMU is a "unique resource," free to keep both its mode of reception and its listening audience. Still, it required the station to negotiate a settlement with its plaintiffs. So, when people complained about the quality or range of WFMU's reception, I countered that the station's signal strength should have been even weaker and was in actuality, truly miraculous. For this, they — and I — were always thankful.

By 1985, our listening audience was growing rapidly. The show enjoyed a reputation for professionalism — measured by the time and effort invested in each broadcast — and community enhancement. The time had come to give "The Hebrew and Jewish Program" a catchier, more recognizable name. And so, we invited our listeners to invent one. Of the thousands of entries we received, we liked "Jewish Music in the Morning" the most. Sitting at the Shabbos table with my father, we came up with *Shirei Shacharit*, a Hebrew name meaning "songs of the morning," and a catchy acronym, *JM in the AM* — and it stuck. Several years later, as the show's format continued to evolve from Jewish music (with occasional guest speakers) to a mix of Jewish music and communal concerns, we tweaked the title again. *JM in the AM* now stood for "Jewish *Moments* in the Morning."

The year 1992 marked the beginning of what I like to call "The Expansion Era." Due to popular demand, *JM in the AM* became a three-hour show, beginning each weekday morning at 6:00 a.m. Then WFMU bought a Catskills, NY radio station that expanded our listening audience tremendously. Each summer, many of our regular listeners head to the Catskills. Thanks to our purchase, their enjoyment of *JM in the AM* continued uninterrupted and as a bonus, several upstate Jewish communities could enjoy the show. In an unexpected development, our show reached several upstate prisons, enabling Jewish inmates to tune in. We are gratified by the many letters we have received from prisoners asserting how meaningful the show is to them.

That same year we launched our afternoon show, broadcast on a fairly weak station from five to seven o'clock, eventually moving to a seven-to-nine pm slot. I created a formatted show, unlike the morning broadcast, that included a nightly newscast, study of *Mishnayos* at designated times, and several weekly spots, such as *Cooking with Chef Baré, From the Grapevine Kosher Wine Spot,* and *Judaica Update*. It seemed to be working; our audience, *Baruch Hashem*, was growing.

Eventually, we needed our own broadcasting studio. Zalman Kopel, known to most listeners as the ever-popular Z.K., had been a loyal volunteer over the years. His technical assistance had been extremely valuable whenever we did a live remote, and I knew that he could handle the job. I hired him to build the studio on the Lower East Side, and he did such a professional job that he was invited to stay on as the show's technical engineer. To this day, I'm always impressed by Zalman's extensive — albeit completely self-taught — technical genius.

It soon became clear that one significant obstacle remained: I hadn't the foggiest idea how to run a business. Fortunately, my brother Yigal, then working for the Jewish Literacy Foundation, came up with a great idea: The two of us could collaborate briefly for our mutual benefit. Specifically, he could teach me what I needed to know to run a business properly, and I could share my contacts to help him network for the Foundation.

When our designated trial run was over, we both realized we had a very successful partnership on our hands; neither of us wanted it to end. Since he had doubled our revenue in merely six months and had what it takes to attract even more quality advertising, I offered Yigal a substantial salary to leave his job at the foundation and work full-time for *The Nachum*

With Gavri at the NSN launch celebration.

Segal Show. Countless people — close relatives, friends, and colleagues — warned us of the dangers of mixing family and business relationships. We were not deterred, and the resulting collaboration has generated only positive results, among them enabling Yigal and his family to fulfill their dream of moving to Israel.

The next major milestone in our program's evolution was the advent of the "Internet era." In 1996, WFMU began putting *JM in the AM* on the Web at www.jmintheam.org. At first, the website only featured the show's live broadcast. Soon enough, however, we began to add our archived broadcasts to the site. To our amazement, www.jmintheam.org was flooded with traffic from all over the world. From Phoenix, Arizona to Geneva, Switzerland and hundreds of places in between, phone calls and emails came pouring in from people who, until the website's launch, had never been able to listen to the show.

Yigal collaborated with the Bottom Line Design Marketing Group to create a website that we named www.NachumSegal.com. *Baruch Hashem*, its popularity was instantaneous, and that popularity continues to grow. After a few years, we could ascertain what features attracted the most traffic, and we have modified the site accordingly. Soon after, the NSN app was developed and immediately became the easiest way to tune in anywhere around the world.

Once Yigal was on board, one of the most significant moves that the network made was hiring Avrumie Finkelstein as Director of Operations. He originally worked remotely from Baltimore and now works remotely from Israel, operating the entire network. He organizes the shows and advertisements, he is the first stop if anything goes wrong technically or programmatically, and he is responsible for everything that goes on behind the scenes. It is virtually impossible to run a network without a reliable, motivated, talented director of operations and I am incredibly grateful to have found Avrumie.

7-year-old Gavri Segal with a wonderful award presented to me by NCSY.

This, and many other photos in this book are credited to Meir Kruter - kruter.com - who has been an integral part of our team for over a decade. He has a shared sense of purpose with our mission of unifying our people. He is also a brilliant artist. His creativity shines through in all his work.

In 2012, Mark Zomick became Director of Projects as we moved into 24-hour programming. Mayer Fertig suggested to Yigal that we must hire Miriam L. Wallach as General Manager of the network to take it to the next level. She immediately named the network NSN, feeling that a new 24-hour effort needed a reliable brand name. She set out to bring in talented hosts who would broaden the network's appeal; that list soon included Naomi Nachman of the Aussie Gourmet, Charlie Harary, Allison Josephs, Michael Fragin, and others who joined our lineup.

Miriam added to the regular schedule of programming by creating major events and live radio broadcasts, such as the Salute to Israel Parade and the Super Bowl Kosher Halftime Show as well as the Jewish Unity Initiatives from Paris, Venice, and Israel. Miriam's ideas and implementations have significantly enhanced the network.

Over the years, my role as a New York radio host has led to other related opportunities. I have been hired to MC many concerts and events and I have had the privilege of announcing the honors at countless weddings. Most recently I was invited to air an English show on Israel's Kol Play station, every Sunday through Wednesday night at six p.m.

I truly felt that I had reached a new career milestone when I planned to visit Jonathan Pollard in prison. The night before the scheduled visit, I was informed that the FBI banned me from going because I was a popular journalist. All my life, I tried to convince people that I was a respectable member of the media and now the FBI declared it to be true!

It is our basic attitude of dedication to the needs of the Jewish community that best explains how we've come to be where we are today. We began very humbly and have attempted to remain so, but we are determined to evolve, taking our cue from that community's ever-changing needs. Listeners often ask why we no longer play certain songs or why our format is different from what it was years ago. Our answer is this: To remain stagnant is to die. Our broadcasts, like every living entity, must constantly grow. Our music, our topics of conversation, and our focus must continue to evolve if we are to reflect the evolution — and needs — of our audience.

FAMILY

To: nachum@wfmu.org

Mazal tov on bringing Yosef into the bris of Avraham and the Jewish People. May he bring you much nachas and grow up like his parents, with a love of Torah, and be a model for all the community.

I do not know if the "virtual bris" I heard on the radio today was a first, but it made me feel like I was right there. Thank you for sharing your simcha with all your listeners, a "virtual family."

While I have had the pleasure of meeting you, I have to believe that through your radio programs you touch so many that my feelings are shared by many.

✳ ✳ ✳

To: nachum@wfmu.org
Subject: Get Well Wishes

Dear Nachum,

I was glad to hear all went well with your son's operation, and I pray he comes home very soon. For you to miss Tuesday's tribute show, it had to be something very important! Happily, all went well.

Best wishes.

To: Nachum@wfmu.org
Subject: I'm Sorry

Nachum, I am so sorry that I couldn't be there with you today. I tried calling, but obviously you weren't answering the phones today. Nachum, the greatest part of the morning was listening to your father — and your interaction with him. I listened with tears in my eyes as he spoke to you with such fatherly pride. And I heard your pride in him as you spoke to him. How blessed you both are.

May you and Staci and each of your Jewels forever be blessed with health, happiness, and parnassa. May you continue to go from strength to strength.

In March 2008, when my parents were told about my upcoming 25th-anniversary celebration and fundraiser at the radio station, my father decided he would join us in person at the studio. At first, I tried to dissuade him; I worried that I would not be able to give him the respect he deserved and I was concerned that I didn't even have a comfortable chair for him. At 91, my father was still driving and going to the gym every day, all while taking care of my infirm mother. But we still wanted to make sure he was cared for properly.

When he insisted on coming to the show, my brother, Rabbi Nate, arranged for someone to drive him. Mattes Weingast introduced him on the air as I would not say his name in front of him. I stood the whole time that he spoke, and I was very careful about respecting him properly in this public forum. My father spoke about the Hebrew letters for 25, כ"ה, standing

With Binyamin Segal

for כבוד ה' and that we had brought honor to G-d through the medium of radio. It was very meaningful not only to me, but also to our audience, that he paid tribute to us on the air.

When he left the studio in Jersey City, he took his car that my brother, Yigal, had driven that morning and started out to run an errand in Livingston, New Jersey. After an hour of not hearing from him, we began to worry, as there had been a heavy downpour, visibility was terrible, and we could not reach him on his cell phone. Yigal and I drove to the Kushner School in Livingston where we expected him to be, and we were informed that he had never arrived.

I called Yanky Meyer *a"h*, founder and director of Misaskim, who told us to immediately go to the Jersey City police department. We sent Yanky and the detectives a digital picture of my father from that morning in the studio and Yanky created a search-and-rescue team with a command center in Jersey City. He got the message out that volunteers were needed and people began pouring in from all over. The detectives, who had originally informed us that they would be leaving at the end of their shift, did not go because they were hesitant to leave when they saw the response and commitment of all the Jewish organizations and hundreds of volunteers.

As the searchers were dispersed throughout the area, television crews began to cover the story. It was moving to see the united effort of people from all communities and backgrounds, joining together to help. Most had never met my father but had heard about him on the air, some were random acquaintances, and some were just people who had heard there were people who needed help and ran to do what they could. There were others who were not available to search but who told me they were saying Tehillim for him or that, in his merit, they had made an effort to do a mitzvah that they otherwise would not have done. To this day, I run into people who tell me they were there searching for my father that night.

By midday on Thursday, we were not sure how long the search would take and began to make contingency plans for Shabbos while Yanky discussed how much we could search on Shabbos. But, the discussion became irrelevant when a local worker spotted a car floating in the Hackensack River. Our family members were driven to the site to identify my father and the search was called off. It seems that he had been driving on a road with no barrier at its end separating it from the river, and with the terrible visibility that morning, he had driven into the water.

He was taken to the regional medical examiner's office in Newark, and they were considering doing a routine autopsy. Ironically, my father, when he had been a rabbi in Newark, years before there were any such laws in place, had fought in that same office, persuading them not to do autopsies on Jewish bodies. Yanky and family friend, Fred Zemel, were both well connected to the examiner's office and asked that nobody touch the rabbi's body until they arrived. How fitting that the same office with which my father had fought for proper ritual according to Jewish law was the same office that ultimately paid the final respect of not interfering with his own proper post-mortem procedures.

The funeral took place on Friday and on Motza'ei Shabbos we flew him to Israel for burial. Another irony that did not escape us was that my father had spent his whole life running away from respect and recognition. A dignified figure whom people naturally looked up to, he was very understated and never wanted recognition. The circumstances of his death attracted much attention, his funerals in New York and in Israel were attended by overflowing crowds, and the *shiva* attracted hundreds from all walks of life.

My fundraiser, which continued after *shiva*, was the most successful ever. Listeners wanted to do whatever they could to help, and many donated in my father's memory. For me, this was a fundraiser that left an indelible impression by the fact that in the last minutes of his life, my father, who was not so effusive with praise throughout his life, had commended and encouraged me publicly.

Seventeen years before my father's sudden death, my mother suffered a near fatal stroke that left her unable to care for herself. Staci and I invited her to move next door to us and we cared for her. Though it's not always easy for a mother-in-law to be living next door, Staci joined me in feeling that it was a privilege to take care of her. We also saw it as a special lesson for our young children, who began to help as they grew older.

As a former refugee who was accustomed to looking over her shoulder in fear, my mother had particular *nachas* when I brought her to meet prominent people. When we visited Gracie Mansion, Mayor Koch spoke to her and made her feel important. Mayor Bloomberg greeted her and joked with her about me. One year at the HASC concert, there was a special tribute to my parents in celebration of their 50th wedding anniversary, which was very meaningful to her.

Many people picture me as someone who sits in a radio studio, talks into a microphone, and wears headphones all day long. Strangers are certainly entitled to think of me this way. After all, I've been headquartered at *JM in the AM* studios for four decades. However, as I learned early on in my career, there is always a story behind every story; nothing is exactly as it seems. In my case, those who really know me — and they include so many of my listeners — know the real story: my parents, my siblings, my wife, and my kids are the keys to my life, both personally and professionally.

The story of my family — the one I grew up in as well as the one I am raising — hardly has the makings of a contemporary bestseller. So why is that story important to recount? Because it influences how I behave as a father, the kind of person I am, and, therefore, the kind of show I broadcast.

It might sound funny coming from someone who everybody knows has been out of the house during universally acknowledged family times: early morning and early evening. However, due to Staci's unfailing patience and my dogged determination, I have found ways to spend significant time with our kids. When my children were young, I rearranged my schedule so that I was home, almost every day, in the late afternoon when the children got home from school, did their homework, and ate their dinner. Sundays are reserved for the family, not as an obligation but as a pleasure. If asked, my kids will tell you that Sunday is my favorite day because I get to spend it all with my family.

There are certain principles of child-rearing that I hold very high. One is that *chesed* begins at home. Before the triplets were born and we had only one child, we were very involved in community service. After they arrived, I opted to discontinue most charity work that required time out of our home. I received calls protesting this decision from organizations where I had volunteered. I explained that I was not detracting from the importance of their cause but that if I had a free hour, I felt strongly that I should spend it bathing and dressing my kids instead of delivering packages to the poor.

My children are certainly aware of what their father does for a living, but I try my hardest to keep my career from infiltrating our family time. When they were young, we overheard our kids discussing whether their father was famous. Finally, they concluded that indeed he was; after all, he appeared on their Uncle Moishy video.

Another guiding principle, this one I learned from my parents, and that Staci and I try our hardest to put into practice, is that children learn by example. When I go to shul despite being exhausted, it is because I saw my own father go to shul despite a high fever or freezing weather. My kids know how serious I am about shul attendance and that we will be going — come rain, sleet, or snow. I believe very strongly that values and traditions are passed down *not* by telling kids what you think they should be doing but by demonstrating how to behave. My kids are well versed in the Segal family football rule: If the weather is such that they would sit outdoors at a football game, then it is weather that they need to go to shul in, as well.

The 4 Segal brothers w/ Soccer Legend, Shep Messing

When I've spoken at any of my children's bar or bat mitzvahs, I've mentioned that the speech is usually the father's opportunity to give his son or daughter advice and direction. However, I added that Staci and I had already been doing that throughout their lives — by example. My children have said that seeing how important Israel is to their parents, Israel has become important to them; that seeing how respectfully their parents treat non-Jews, they have learned to do the same. (They also describe how annoying it is to attend events with a father who is always running into people he knows…but that can be the subject of their own books.)

Looking back at my own childhood, I recall how my parents raised us with very distinct values and ideals but, at the same time, with the ability to think and act independently. I have five siblings, Leah, Moshe *a"h*, Chaim Nate, Peninah, and Yigal. Anyone who knows the six of us knows that we are vastly different from one another. Still, in our own individual way, each of us has incorporated the strong morals of our parents. From the beginning of our life together, Staci and I have tried to follow their example. We believe it is of the utmost importance to teach our children to take responsibility for their rooms, for their actions — and for themselves.

My parents' generation was one that would have naturally looked down at someone who chose a career in radio. The first time that I told my father about my radio show at YU, I was worried about his reaction. He really took interest in what I told him and asked questions about it. As a gifted public speaker, my father was able to appreciate the ability that I had to speak to so many people at once. And, as a shul rabbi, at the time in the largest shul in New Jersey, he had always inculcated in us the value of using our time productively, not to prioritize making money, but to use our time to help the community. Though he would say it half-jokingly, it was so meaningful when I would hear that he had said to someone, "I used to be Rabbi Zev Segal, now I am known as Nachum Segal's father."

My oldest brother, Moshe, served to bridge part of the generation gap, filling many important roles and acting as a father figure by playing ball with me, taking me on trips, and offering me much-appreciated advice. He took this role very seriously and we were very close. On the Sunday before he died, I went to visit him in the hospital. He said something to me that I will never forget: "I'll always be proud to be a Segal, but I am especially proud to be your brother."

At the funeral, the rabbi began to tear my shirt on the left side, the side reserved for a parent's death. I told the rabbi to switch to my right side, the side torn for other close relatives. But I found it meaningful, as I had always said that Moshe was like a father to me.

Staff members and listeners alike have told me time and again that the show's familial feeling can be explained by one fact: Family is very important to me. Whether it is the feeling of connection among vastly different listeners or the strong bond between the audience and my personal family, I could not have imagined doing the show in any other way.

Our *sheva brachos* was broadcast live, as was the *bris* of our triplet, Yosef. The audience's sincere joy for me and my family was moving beyond description. In particular, the birth of the triplets received worldwide attention; it was covered by the *New York Daily News*, and many people donated $54 at the fundraiser soon after their birth (three times 18/chai) in honor of these miracle babies. People whom I didn't even know said that our joy felt like their own family *simcha*. How could we not share our celebration with them, our extended family? The broadcasts of our *simchas* allowed us to do just that. People often stop me and say they will never forget those broadcasts. It makes me so happy to have helped create this feeling of family among so many people who used to be strangers.

More than anything else, the values my parents instilled in me dictate the content of my broadcasts. The importance of the State of Israel, of helping all types of people, of Jewish unity and pride — these are the ideals I was brought up with, these are the ideals I try to instill in my children, but, of particular significance to my listening audience, these are the ideals that prompt what I decide to air on the show. They also dictate how I regard my work. My parents taught me to take everything I do seriously. Each show deserves the proper amount of preparation, each live remote deserves meticulous attention, and each guest deserves unconditional respect.

Raising six children is certainly not easy. Each time we flew to Israel and presented the security agent with all our passports, I got a look that seemed to say, "Six kids, including triplets? These guys must be crazy!" Caring for triplets, especially at the beginning, was particularly challenging. When they came home from the hospital, almost three months after they were born, I took a week off from work. On the Monday morning that I returned to the studio, I passed through the living room where they were sleeping, each hooked up to monitors and machines. Our house looked like a hospital; I must admit, I felt physically ill trying to figure out how we were going to get through this stage.

Now, years later, it is amazing to see how the values we instilled have come to fruition. The kids have gravitated towards friends with shared values of Judaism, Israel, Torah, and mitzvah observance. It is amazing to see one's kids who have incorporated the values we tried to impart and who have married spouses of whom we are very proud.

I look back with unending gratitude for the family I was lucky to grow up in and the family that I have been blessed to raise. Both have given me

With Chava, Yehoshua, Yosef and their MDS pals

With Chava and Yonina

constant support. Both have taught me life-enhancing lessons. I only hope and pray that I will use those lessons to become a better radio host, a better person, a better son and brother, a better husband to Staci, and a better father to Binyamin, Chava, Yosef, Yehoshua, Yonina, and Gavriel, their spouses, and our grandchildren.

With Yehoshua and Yosef

JEWISH MUSIC

To: nachum@wfmu.org
Subject: JEWISH MUSIC

Please excuse my perhaps somewhat too spontaneous comment on the songs played this morning on your show. But as one who davened with Ben Zion Shenker for many years and one who admires the nigunim and songs of Avraham Fried, Dedi…, it appears as if this style of Jewish music is too far removed from the traditional heartfelt tunes to which to expose our children. I do indeed realize the value of such music to certain segments of your listening audience, and it is certainly impossible to please all the diverse segments of that audience. However, I'm not sure that the holy words of our Shabbos nigunim should be applied to melodies that sound like tunes of the Beach Boys.

To: nachum@wfmu.org
Subject: JEWISH MUSIC

I guess I'll just plead for better musical taste. Don't play everything new that comes out, because most of it is (musically) trash; avoid the type of loud noise that some new artists put out, surrounding their great voices with really ugly accompaniments. Please concentrate on groups and individuals with proven musical taste, such as the Rabbis' Sons, Safam, Chava Alberstein, even (in most cases) Dveykus. Many groups and individuals started out with good taste in production, but then succumbed to the popular malady. And what happened to Arkady? I haven't heard him lately, and his music is fabulous.

❋ ❋ ❋

To: Nachum@wfmu.org
Subject: Oif Simchas

This is regarding the two callers on Monday who had such great distress about Oif Simchas. It pains me that people are so narrow that if a type of music does not fit their concept of "frum," it is therefore no good. My entire family (three generations) LOVES Oif Simchas, loved the concert at Manhattan Center, and can't wait for the third album to come out.

Incidentally, the choreography was professional, excellent, and uplifting. There was nothing lewd or anti-"frum" about it. If MBD were to sing the same songs, I'll bet the music would then be deemed OK.

I would greatly appreciate it if you would forward this message to Shea Mendlowitz and/or Oif Simchas. I hope you continue to play Oif Simchas on your shows!!

❋ ❋ ❋

To: nachum@wfmu.org
Subject: mizrach may

First of all, I just want to thank you for MOST of your programming. I appreciate the fact that one can listen to Jewish music on the radio and on the web.

Having said that, I must object to the "mizrach may" programming. The name of your program is "Jewish Moments in the Morning." How do you define Israeli rock music as "Jewish"? Is it just because the artists are Jewish? Would you play Bob Dylan's music or Barbra Streisand's? I can tolerate it if the words of the songs were from Tanach, Talmud, etc., or even if they deal on an ad hoc basis with Judaism (as many of the "Hasidic" English or Yiddish songs do). But these pure Israeli rock/pop songs have no place on your show.

Furthermore, I recall R' Dovid Goldwasser stating one could give maaser money to support your show. Can you justify maaser money being spent to support the dissemination of the songs mentioned above? I don't see how you can.

Subject: MIZRACH MAY
To: NACHUM@wfmu.org

DEAR NACHUM;
I'M WRITING JUST TO LET YOU KNOW THAT THIS MORNING'S PROGRAM WAS PHENOMENAL. THE MUSIC WAS BEAUTIFUL, MANY OF THE SONGS WERE QUITE NOSTALGIC AND ALL IN ALL IT WAS A THOROUGHLY ENJOYABLE MORNING. I WISH YOU WOULD INTERSPERSE "ISRAELI" MUSIC INTO YOUR PROGRAM MORE OFTEN.

On a crisp autumn night in September 1981, I took my first steps into the studio of WYUR, Yeshiva University's radio station, to host what I hoped would be the first of many Jewish music shows. I was thrilled. I was excited. The only problem was that I did not know the first thing about Jewish music.

Aside from an occasional listen to Shlomo Carlebach's tunes, my exposure to Jewish music was practically nonexistent. What motivated me to broadcast Jewish music? Simply this: When I saw how many WYUR applicants wanted to host shows featuring American popular music, I figured that if I picked a different musical category, my chances would improve. Luckily for me, my roommate Elchanan Wasserman had an extensive knowledge of contemporary Jewish singers.

Before that first night on the air, I begged Elchanan to accompany me to the studio. He finally acquiesced and sat next to me throughout the show, choosing which songs to play and in which sequence. Unfortunately for me, the second show took place during YU's annual Chanukah concert and no amount of pleading would convince him to join me at the station. On my own, I did the only thing that someone who did not know the difference between Mordechai Ben David and Dveykus could do. I played the exact same songs, in the exact same order, as I had played the previous week. It was the best I could do and I just hoped that no one would notice.

Several years have passed since those first ignorant nights on the air. Ironically, I have not only gained a working knowledge of and a wholehearted appreciation for contemporary Jewish music, but I have found myself at the very center of its development. As an active participant in the process, I have been privileged to witness firsthand both the industry's advancement and its audience's proliferation.

In the show's early years, the population of Jewish music fans was relatively small. It was less likely for someone under the age of twenty to listen to Jewish music. Concerts featuring Jewish artists were few and far between, and they were predominantly for the benefit of one neighborhood or a specific institution.

The first major events that I was asked to host were the Diaspora Yeshiva Band's farewell concerts in late 1983. Its following was exuberant yet, by today's standards, small. My big break came when my friend, Rabbi Azriel Siff, encouraged the concerts' organizer, Moish Rosenbaum, to hire "that new WFMU DJ" to serve as MC. Those were exciting nights at Brooklyn College and Queens College; the band attracted enthusiastic crowds.

A really big turning point in the Jewish music industry came in January of 1988, when the first HASC concert took place. In one night, Sheya

(L-R) Menachem Herman, Ben Zion Solomon, Ruby Harris, Avraham Rosenblum & Gedaliah Goldstein (Diaspora Yeshiva Band members).

The Rabbi's Sons Reunion Concert. One of my favorite MC gigs.

With my late great friend Sheya Mendlowitz, a great Jewish Music Producer

Mendlowitz and David "Ding" Golding transformed our community's attitude toward Jewish music and Jewish performances. By raising the bar in so many ways — renting Lincoln Center's Avery Fisher Hall, charging a minimum of $50 per ticket, producing a top-notch show featuring the finest artists of the day — they forced the world to take notice of a burgeoning industry. People who had never attended a Jewish concert were there. Due to its overwhelming success, that evening produced a ripple effect; almost immediately, Jewish concerts began popping up all over the place.

With Sheya Mendlowitz

I did not MC the first few HASC concerts, but in 1991 I was asked to and was delighted to accept the invitation. It's a thrill to meet so many phenomenal performers, to look into the audience at HASC and so many other concerts I have been privileged to MC throughout the years, and to see the array of people all coming together to hear what has become high-quality Jewish music. When thinking back to the way it was when I started out, I sometimes can't believe how accepted it has become for all types of people —from the ultra-Orthodox to the unaffiliated — to attend these events.

Following the HASC concert wakeup call of 1988, we witnessed an explosion of unique artists who succeeded in forming Jewish music into the vastly popular forms we enjoy today. Numerous genres appeared on the scene, each appealing to a different segment of the community, each generating a number of listeners that had previously been unimaginable. It has been fascinating to host many of these artists and to hear what they think about new musical trends and the new listeners coming on the scene.

Beginning with Mordechai Ben David's revolutionary album, *Let My People Go*, in 1984, listeners were introduced to a new, modern sound. The title track's unifying political message appealed to many, including people who would not otherwise listen to Jewish music. MBD, as well as Avraham Fried, took classic Jewish concepts and adjusted them to meet the changing interests of the community — an artistic method that has certainly withstood the test of time, as indicated by the fact that these artists have been at the top of the industry for four decades.

A short time later, many artists began offering quality songs that, like those of Mordechai Ben David and Avraham Fried, attracted listeners seeking spiritually uplifting music. Choirs and singers drew in those who were

With Mordechai Ben David

impressed that Orthodox Jewish musicians and artists could perform so skillfully.

Different artists had different styles that appealed to different types of people, some were appreciated by younger listeners and some by older, some were culled from secular music and some were strictly Chassidic. Dedi, Yerachmiel Begun and his Miami Boys Choir, Yaakov Shwekey and others stepped through the door that their predecessors had opened, and they created a much larger and more diverse listening base. More recently, we've seen the new phenomenon of Ishai Ribo and other Israeli artists who have universal appeal. Today, it would not be hard to find an Israeli soccer team listening to the same song being played in Orthodox circles.

In addition, some wanted to reach Jewish hearts with meaningful, beautiful lyrics in English. For those who were less familiar with Hebrew but still wanted religiously themed songs, Abie Rotenberg of Journeys and Lenny Solomon of Shlock Rock have had a huge impact. With beauty and sophistication, Rotenberg's recordings have brought the genre to a whole new level and Shlock Rock has put new words to old pop tunes in such a clever way that kids (and adults) don't even realize how much they are learning from them.

One of the most meaningful observations of my radio work occurred when Mrs. Chaya Newman, principal of a prominent local yeshiva high school, thanked *JM in the AM* for "making it cool for teenagers to listen to Jewish music." The events and artists of the late 80s and early 90s are what produced this dramatic change. Our show was proud to be the conduit for their vision and talent.

By promoting concerts on the air, we have played a role in the success of Jewish music events. By featuring new artists who would otherwise have difficulty gaining exposure, we have contributed to the development of the Jewish music industry. From the very beginning of our broadcasting history, due to the sheer volume of people we reach, we've been considered one of the best ways to get the word out about upcoming Jewish events. There have even been events so minor, or of interest to such a small segment of our community, that we have asked why their organizers want to have them announced. The answer we have received is this: Even if the announcement convinces nobody to come to the event, it should still be broadcast just to lend it substance and credibility. In fact, in the September 2000 *New York Times* article about the show, one listener was quoted as saying, "If it's not on *JM in the AM*, it didn't happen."

Even today, with the plethora of avenues where one can obtain and listen to Jewish music, many artists feel that if *JM in the AM* ignores them, it will be harder for them to gain popularity. The signature interview when a singer debuted an album on *JM in the AM* would be the unique way to alert fans to its release. Artists still feel it is important to appear on the show among their other platforms and we are the address for listeners to hear interesting conversations with Jewish music stars — past, present, and future. I have watched the evolution of musical recordings from records to cassettes to CDs to MP3s and now to online access. While music is readily available to our community on many other platforms, we still get constant requests to play certain songs. Listening on the radio creates a sense of community; people like to know that they are listening to a song together with others in all parts of the world.

I am committed to broadcasting what listeners want to hear. At the same time, I make programming decisions based on my belief that specific songs have contributed to the recent surge in Jewish pride and identity. I think listening to and creating Jewish music can only lead to good things. There are those who object to borrowing genres from the secular world and presenting them with Jewish themes. From the plethora of calls and emails I receive on this topic, it is clear that everyone has a different definition as to what qualifies as a Jewish song. I like to say, "Everyone has their own playlist."

I think that the ever-changing world of Jewish music elevates the profane and makes it holy. I think it allows our youth to express their creativity in a more positive way than they otherwise would. I think it spreads interest in Jewish music and Judaism in general. And I'm excited to be a part of that world and to play whatever role I can to help it grow.

JEWISH HEROES

To: Nachum@wfmu.org
Subject: Dudu Fisher

I heard the broadcast when Dudu Fisher spoke about how hard it was to miss the anniversary show of Les Misérables, but I didn't have the chance to call in and wish him a Yasher Koach. Pirkei Avot teaches us that according to the suffering, so is the reward, and for his mesirut nefesh he will certainly, after many years, be making a l'chaim on the wine that was bottled in the Garden of Eden. Chazak v'ematz!

To: nachum@wfmu.org

Dear Nachum:
Your interview with Dudu Fisher and Avrohom Fried this morning was one of your best. It is absolutely AMAZING what I, as an "FFB," take for granted. That caller, who said it is not a choice whether or not to work on Shabbos, is correct. However, he failed to realize that although it is not a choice for him, it can be a test for others. If I may say so, your answer to him hit the nail on the head: that you hope he would never have to face such a test.

We pray every day that G-d will not bring us "lo leidei nisoyon," face to face with a test. Sometimes we fail to understand the importance of that prayer. I just want to say that I respect Dudu Fisher even more after this morning. Not for his musical talents alone, but for his mesirus nefesh to be an observant Jew.

Keep up the great work!!

Heroism, particularly of the Jewish kind, can be defined in so many ways. Are our heroes those Jews who have made the greatest impact on the world? Or, do we choose to admire those who have had the most influence on our religious practices? Do we honor those fellow Jews who have achieved the greatest success in their fields? Or, do we hold in the highest regard those who assist the greatest number of Jewish people? Many of us, at various points in our lives, have looked up to different types of people and it is important, I think, to answer these questions. In other words, we need to determine who our heroes are in order to identify for ourselves and for our children what we truly value.

While I agree with all these definitions of heroism, and I am the first to laud the Torah giant, the Israeli soldier, and other such heroes, I enjoy broadening the definition of Jewish heroism. In my mind, there are great Jewish heroes who should be recognized and looked up to for making difficult choices between career dreams and Torah values — and have made a *Kiddush Hashem* by courageously choosing a Torah way of life despite the allure of secular fame. These are our unsung heroes who, through seemingly mundane activities, show true Jewish heroism and justly deserve our respect.

If I did not realize it before, I certainly know now that this criterion is not universally accepted. Over the years, the heroes I have featured on my shows have generated mixed reactions. Many have applauded my selections, recognizing the difficulties these people have encountered and the strength it took to make such a *Kiddush Hashem*. Others can't relate to the struggle, maintaining that the choice is a simple, unremarkable one; they ask rhetorically, "Who would ever consider violating Shabbos?" Many callers have asked why some people place themselves in such challenging situations, and, in turn, why I am publicizing those who do.

Why? Because I truly believe that within Judaism there are many role models from whom we can learn. Because I know that the athlete or actor who has successfully overcome the biggest challenge of his or her life could be telling the most inspiring story my listeners have ever heard. And, because I maintain that the seemingly simple declaration, "Shabbos is more important than anything else in the world," deserves to be recognized for the huge *Kiddush Hashem* that it is.

Years ago I interviewed David Fishof, someone I consider a hero. He has been an agent for professional athletes as famous as Phil Simms and musicians such as Ringo Starr and Roger Daltrey. David is, in my eyes, a walking *Kiddush Hashem*. Here is someone who spends most of his days and nights interacting with rock and roll stars, celebrities who attract millions of people to their concerts and whose popularity is worth millions upon millions of dollars. And yet, anyone who tuned in to *JM in the AM* and heard David describe his experiences at the Boyaner Rebbe's *tisch* in Yerushalayim cannot deny what really matters to him. His job, Fishof explains, allows him to express his creativity. Booking tours for the stars is what he's good at. But while in his car or his hotel room, he's listening to the music of Avraham Fried. For teenagers, or even adults, struggling to define themselves and their priorities, David's message is incontrovertible.

Fishof's clients, many of whom would never otherwise have had the opportunity to know an Orthodox Jew, have developed a keen respect for their agent and his Shabbos observance. David shared with our listeners several stories of multi-million-dollar negotiations that stopped in their tracks because Shabbos was approaching. He would calmly explain that the talks would have to resume on Saturday night. While negotiating a contract for Phil Simms, the team's representative called incessantly, insisting it was an emergency that the quarterback be signed that day, Saturday. He soon learned that there is no sports emergency or concert engagement — regardless of the sum of money involved — that will prompt David Fishof to work on Shabbos. In a world of dubious morals and erratic values, Fishof truly stands out as someone steadfast in his Torah principles, creating a good name for himself and for Jews around the world.

Among the many I've interviewed, three sports figures stand out as role models not only for their athletic prowess but for their integrity. They are Dmitriy Salita, Tamir Goodman, and Beatie Deutsch.

Former welterweight boxing champion Dmitriy Salita's famous quote, "If anyone wants a whupping from me, they've gotta wait until after sundown," and the clause in his contract stating that he wouldn't fight on Shabbos, had a seismic impact on the boxing world. He explained to our listeners that the worst thing a boxer can do to his body is spend an entire day refraining from exercise. But he knew that it would harm him far more to exercise on Shabbos. And so, he rested throughout those twenty-five hours, secure in his conviction that he would be successful because he had chosen correctly.

To me, Salita's most impressive feat is his proclamation to the press: "I will never compromise my beliefs. Never. It's not a question. I have a personal relationship with G-d that I won't compromise. My boxing is such a big part of my life, but it won't get in the way of my religion. It can't, and it won't."

When the University of Maryland expressed interest in basketball sensation Tamir Goodman, he made it crystal clear that he would not play on Shabbos. The university and the entire ACC Conference were prepared to revamp their schedules to accommodate him. When he wore a yarmulke to play basketball in otherwise completely secular leagues, fans took notice, and as one coach put it, "The kid who stood up for something he believed in." When he appeared in *Sports Illustrated* in a full-page photo wearing *tefillin*, it was a truly eye-opening moment for the millions of readers of the preeminent sports magazine. But Tamir didn't understand what all the fuss was about. "This is just who I am," he explained.

Beatie Deutsch, a charedi mother of five from Israel, is an elite runner who has won several Israeli and international marathons. She has continuously served as a role model by showing the world her clear priorities, shattering expectations by winning races with her head covered and being modestly dressed. With dreams to represent Israel in the Olympics, she trained vigorously, even through a pregnancy. She qualified for the Olympics, ranking as one of the top 80 women runners in the world. But, unlike athletes in many other sports, Deutsch is dependent on the world's schedule to reach her goals and when the Tokyo Olympics was postponed due to Covid, the women's marathon moved from a Sunday to a Saturday. She tried to appeal the date, but when she lost, she pulled out of the race and showed the world what we mean when we say that our lives are completely guided by our faith, explaining, "I'm proud that I can still pursue my dreams without sacrificing my values."

For those who look up to professional athletes — and there are certainly a significant number of us who do — these people represent Jewish heroism, because they knew how much easier the sporting life would be if they compromised their beliefs. And still, they have used their status and influence to inspire others in the Jewish community, and the world, by saying that G-d is first and foremost; that religious commitment is uncompromising.

During the 2004 Democratic National Convention, I was able to pull Elly Libin away from his work just long enough to learn what he does for the convention's television audience. Libin, the man responsible for much of the technology behind broadcasts of the Super Bowl, the US Open, the presidential inaugurations, and many other high-profile events, is as scrupulous in his religious observance as he is in his technological professionalism. Although constantly surrounded by lavish non-kosher buffets for the networks' important guests, Libin is content with eating a bag of potato chips in another room.

Elly is especially meticulous when it comes to matters of religious integrity. Two days before the 1988 Democratic National Convention in Atlanta, a technological emergency developed. That day happened to be Shabbos. Knowing he couldn't be reached by phone, a member of Elly's staff drove over to his hotel to get him. Unwilling to make excuses or leniencies, Elly walked several miles to the Omni Arena, in almost one hundred-degree heat, to talk his colleagues through the solution.

Senator Joseph Lieberman became, perhaps, the most famous Orthodox Jew in the country when he ran for Vice President in 2000. There were countless photographs of him walking to shul and numerous articles about his special requests for kosher food. It was as if running for public office while still maintaining personal standards and values was an anomaly. On *JM in the AM*, he told us how, in 1988, when Connecticut's Democratic Party re-nominated him for U.S. Senator, he missed his own nominating convention because it took place on *Simchat Torah*.

In more recent years, Jason Greenblatt, Special Representative for International Negotiations for President Trump, took his role as representative of the Jewish people very seriously, wearing his yarmulke in all places and declaring clearly that Hashem is more important to him than politics. On his first overseas trip with Trump, he was expected to fly with him aboard Air Force One. But, as the situation was not life-threatening, he would not fly with him on Shabbos. Instead, he flew early on Thursday, spent a very lonely Shabbos in Saudi Arabia, and was available to begin working with the President as soon as Shabbos was over.

During the summer of 2022, Greenblatt was saying *Kaddish* for his mother. Finding himself in a remote location in Saudi Arabia, he gathered a minyan of his Jewish group and proceeded to daven Mincha with many Muslim onlookers. A short while later, he found himself in a meeting in Jerusalem with Prime Minister Netanyahu. When he needed to leave early to say *Kaddish* on his mother's yahrzeit, Netanyahu offered to gather a minyan and davened together with him.

Recently, I interviewed two young professionals who are impressive not only for what they have accomplished in their fields but also for the message they have sent about not working on Shabbos. Ari Meirov has 70,000 followers on Twitter (now X) who read his up-to-the minute NFL updates. At the beginning of his online venture, people did not understand how someone whose livelihood depends on staying up to date can turn everything off for twenty-five hours. But, over the years, they have learned to respect Ari's principles. When the NFL draft goes into Friday night, Ari will fly to Seattle so he can get an extra three hours of posting and then spend Shabbos in Seattle.

But, regardless of where he is, once Shabbos starts, he does not even think about football. Busy with family or friends, davening, and keeping Shabbos properly, he does not worry about what he is missing or wish he could be posting. The NFL is so enormous and so well-funded that it is accustomed to being the strongest and getting what it wants. But Ari Meirov has declared to all who know him that Shabbos is more important than the NFL.

Eli Lunzer, founder of Eli Lunzer Productions, specializes in brand marketing and event productions for celebrities, athletes, charities, and corporations. In our interview, Eli emphasized that his colleagues respect his decision to spend a day away from his work surrounded by friends, family, and spirituality. In addition to respecting him, he explained that many have expressed the feeling that he is lucky to do that and they are envious that they do not have this opportunity. At the minimum, they would love to have a reason to shut their phones for twenty-four hours. "We say *no* to events that we can't execute 100 percent." He explains that he has had to give up major opportunities because of the limits posed by Shabbos observance. But he feels that Shabbos, friends, and family are all that he needs.

A moving account of Jewish heroism was shared during an interview with world-renowned singer, Dudu Fisher. Fisher is a man who worked all his life to achieve success on the stage. After working his way up through the ranks, he achieved one of the most coveted theatrical roles: the lead in Broadway's *Les Misérables*. Dudu's contract featured an iron-clad clause: The star of the show would not perform on Shabbat or Yom Tov. He would jokingly say that on the understudy's dressing room door, the sign read, "Shabbos Goy."

In what would have been a peak moment in his career, Fisher was invited to participate in the *Les Misérables* Tenth Anniversary Dream Cast in Concert at London's Royal Albert Hall, featuring all the musical's previous stars. Months before the 1995 performance was to take place, its producer proudly called Fisher to say, "Because I know you won't perform on Friday night, and because everyone involved really wants you to be a part of this spectacular event, we went out of our way and switched around the schedule to ensure that it will take place on a weeknight." It took Dudu just a few minutes to realize that he was facing a tremendous dilemma: The weeknight the producer had so considerately chosen fell on the first night of Sukkot.

Dudu described the turmoil, the soul searching, the questions that assaulted him: What if he walked to the theater? What if he shared the microphone with a non-Jew? Would these or any other permutations enable him to fulfill his artistic dream?

Ultimately, Dudu knew he could have appeared onstage and made sure not to violate the holiday. He knew he could have justified that appearance, considering all that the producers had done to accommodate him. But he also knew that a Sukkot appearance on the stage of London's Royal Albert Hall would not be in the true spirit of the holiday.

Dudu will forever be asking himself, "What if?" because, in the end, he spent the holiday with his family in their *sukkah* in Petach Tikva. This message of priorities, of commitment and of sacrifice for Torah values, made a huge impression not only on me but on thousands of our listeners. It is a message of crystal-clear integrity that has been absorbed by all of Dudu's children, each strong adherents to the values of Torah and Eretz Yisrael. I've often seen Dudu shake his head in wonderment when contemplating those wonderful children. His words are a testament to his modesty: "I don't know where I went right."

I can certainly relate personally to each and every one of these interviews. As many who knew me in 1982 can attest, there was a period in my life when I was down, certain that I'd have to choose between radio and religion. I couldn't fathom how I could break into an industry — an industry that I had dreamed of all my life — in which working on Shabbos is such a given.

Furthermore, I had just seen two good friends struggling with this very dilemma, each reaching a dramatically different resolution. During my last year at Yeshiva University's WYUR, they were my colleagues. We all shared the same lifelong dream: to work in radio. Our experiences at WYUR only served to foster these ambitions. Both friends received coveted internships in local stations' sports departments — Robert Katz at NBC, my other colleague at Sportschannel. Apparently, their aspirations were not unfounded because, soon enough, each was offered a job at their respective stations. The only problem was that both jobs mandated that they work on Shabbos.

Robert opted to uphold his religious convictions. In doing so, he knew he would have to choose a completely different career. He knew he would be giving up all that he had ever dreamed of doing, but he would not have it any other way.

Today, Robert is a colleague on our *JM in the AM* staff. Our other friend accepted the job offer and is still involved in the media world but, unfortunately, he is no longer Torah observant.

Being able to empathize fully with Robert, who certainly would have been a Major League announcer had it not been for Shabbos, his story left me with mixed emotions in 1982. The prospect of having to make the same choice saddened me. Nevertheless, I was inspired, realizing that I had just gotten my first glimpse of true Jewish heroism. I wondered what it was about each of my presumably similar friends that had led them on such diametrically different paths.

I once asked my father why he and his siblings had all remained observant despite the rampant assimilation their generation had faced. He answered with an anecdote about his mother. She had arrived in America on Shabbos and, in order to get off the boat, she needed to sign certain forms. It had been an arduous two-week journey. Her accompanying children were impatient to disembark. She knew that she could have relied upon a halachic dispensation to sign the papers. But she adamantly refused. Until nightfall, she and her children sat on the dock with their luggage. She demonstrated that there is nothing more important in the world than Shabbos. My father felt that it was her attitude that led his entire family to remain religious, even under difficult conditions.

Stories of everyday people like my grandmother are what inspire me most. Stories of people who have not had the luxury to spend their days in sheltered Jewish environments. Stories of people who face challenges to their religious convictions almost every single day. These men and women, who make ongoing sacrifices for the sake of Torah, who maintain uncompromising standards regarding kashrut, Torah study, and interpersonal behavior — they are the true role models for our next generation.

Thank G-d, in my own life, I never did have to face these challenges head on. I've been blessed with a successful career in radio that enabled me to live a fully Orthodox Jewish life. Still, I wonder what leads people to the decisions they make and what ultimately gives them the strength to choose Torah over something else they also love. After becoming a father, these thoughts preoccupy me more than ever. What are the traits that lead a person to make heroic decisions, and how can I successfully instill those traits in my children?

These questions, of course, have more than one answer. But I think that the best way to produce people who are willing to act heroically is to publicize their achievements, their sacrifices, and their strength of character. I'm working on it.

PARTNERSHIPS

Over the many years of my career, I have had a wide variety of guests, thousands of them, on the air. It is so hard to predict how an interview will turn out. I've had several instances where I invited a great lecturer or dynamic personality and the interview was mediocre. At the same time, people I had thought were quieter or more private surprised me with intriguing stories and anecdotes, making the interview very exciting.

But there are some guests who surpass all expectations and I have come to refer to them as partners. Partners, by definition, help each other, and these guests do not merely promote their causes and entertain listeners. Instead, their relationship with me and our chemistry on the air create what I like to call "Radio Magic." Our conversations are so compelling that the resulting whole is clearly greater than the sum of its parts, as they make me a better radio host and the show a far better show. Some examples:

Rabbi Yehoshua (Josh) Fass

Yehoshua Fass, the founder of Nefesh B'Nefesh, is an amazing partner in our show's quest to promote *aliyah* and to encourage and guide North American Jewry to make living in Israel a priority. The fact that we are two people coming from such different vantage points makes our conversations even more engaging. Josh, someone who took the mission and dream of *aliyah* and transformed it into a reality, is speaking to me, who has been preaching for decades on the importance of moving to Israel, but has not made a significant move in that direction. That background and the fact that Josh finds in me a responsible Jewish leader who has convinced many to make *aliyah* has solidified our partnership and enhanced our on-air mission tremendously.

Though Yehoshua and I are both very busy with our communal and family responsibilities, once a year, we fly together on the Nefesh B'Nefesh summer charter flight, giving us the opportunity to discuss his latest initiatives and my latest approaches to speaking to my audience about *aliyah*. These conversations are always gratifying and validating. I try to encourage him to the greatest degree possible and he in turn, encourages me to continue publicizing the beauty and the significance of the Land and State of Israel.

One of my favorite expressions is, "The future of the Jewish People is in the State of Israel." Rabbi Fass and I are able to transmit the importance of this mantra with an on-air partnership that is greater than either of us could do alone. Our enthusiasm and passion for Israel in addition to his Torah and practical approaches to *aliyah* results in listeners and their families keeping Israel at the top of their list of priorities.

Chaim Silber *a"h*

Chaim Silber, known to many as Lobo, spent his life trying to find ways to help others and make life more enjoyable for everyone. In addition to being a generous philanthropist to all types of causes, he enjoyed doing seemingly small things that made a difference. On the fun side, he would hire an ice cream truck for children in the bungalow colony and when boys came to his home to collect money on Purim, he invited them to his backyard basketball court and told them he would donate according to how many foul shots they scored. But, he was serious about his giving as well, and was very involved with couples who had difficulties with infertility and other serious circumstances.

Nachum w/ Chaim "Lobo" Silber A"H

Lobo would join me on the air to discuss such disparate topics as the bungalow baseball league; the ability of all, regardless of income, to help others; and the importance of having a list of people to call on Erev Shabbos. Over the years, these conversations developed into fun and inspiring radio segments that people still talk about today.

Chaim was an important partner in thinking of creative ways to put smiles on people's faces and he was the first person I would invite on the show when I wanted to talk about chesed initiatives. He helped transform our Elul and Nissan campaigns from just raising money for food and clothing to also buying tickets for Chol HaMoed trips for underprivileged families. He believed strongly that affordability should not prevent any child from having a good time on Chol HaMoed or any down time during the year.

Rabbi Mordechai Kanelsky

Rabbi Kanelsky was born in Moscow, and though he barely spoke English when he first came on the show, his bubbly, upbeat personality has always led to incredibly entertaining on-air conversations that would probably fall flat with any other guest. He often speaks about his years of hiding in Moscow basements to learn Torah and jokes with me about where he went on Chol HaMoed trips (not Six Flags) as a child. He describes living in Communist Russia, where, one year, the government purposely delayed the matzah shipment from America until after Pesach. That year, the community celebrated Pesach Sheni and then put the matzah away for the following year to guarantee they would have matzah at the next Seder.

One of the most profound stories he ever told on the air is that of his mother-in-law in Russia, who traveled for hours by train to go to the *mikvah*. Once, when she arrived, it was full of glass and she spent the night emptying, cleaning, and refilling it. She did all this knowing that her family would have no clue where she was and knowing that she would miss the last train back home. This story inspired a listener to tell us that, after hearing of the type of sacrifice the rabbi's mother-in-law made for the mitzvah of *mikvah*, he realized how ridiculous it is that he hesitates before eating bread because of the added "burden" of washing and bentching.

When you have a radio partner who brings great material to the microphone; along with a sense of humor and chemistry with the host, you will often strike radio gold. Listeners have told me that they will not get out of their car until the conversation with Rabbi Kanelsky is over. Guests like him, who eventually become on-air partners, have the qualities to turn a regular interview or conversation into a fascinating encounter.

Rabbi Dovid Heber

When Rabbi Heber, author of *The Intriguing World of Jewish Time*, is on the air, he brings out my passion for Jewish calendar trivia. We can explore topics that others might have found boring or complex and confusing, but together we bring them to life in a clear, easy-to-understand manner. He has a more scholarly angle while I offer a layman's view, but our joint enthusiasm for the topic makes for gripping radio conversation.

Many listeners have shared that if they miss a segment with Rabbi Heber, they go back to the archives to listen so as not to miss out on such interesting programming. We even have listeners who go to the archives to review the conversation to ensure that they get every nuance of Rabbi Heber's conversations.

With Meir Weingarten. Boy do I miss him!

If you want to know if we will be making an *eruv tavshilin* in the upcoming year, if Rosh Chodesh Teves will be one day or two, or when is the next year that we will lack double *parshiyos*, then you must listen to the conversations I have had with Rabbi Heber. These are just some examples of the exciting trivia we discuss and how the combination of his knowledge and my enthusiasm works together to create great radio.

Meir Weingarten a"h

The stories of my career, of *JM in the AM* or of the Nachum Segal Network, cannot be told without including the integral role that was played by Meir Weingarten. When Meir and I were together on the air, broadcasting our shared mission of imparting a love of Israel to our listeners, there was a certainty that our two voices had a greater impact than either of us could ever accomplish alone. Somehow, our shared message became more inspiring, more educational, and more entertaining.

We referred to ourselves as Joshua and Caleb, referencing that we were those who were telling the truth about Israel. So strong was our bond that when Meir left us so suddenly, I was not sure that Joshua could continue the mission without Caleb, and I spent many shows trying to create a new reality without him.

I first met Meir in 1989; within months we had forged such a strong friendship, based on our common backgrounds and values, that I chose him to be a witness under my *chuppah*. Though I had many other friends whom I had known longer, my connection with Meir felt brotherly.

I would bring Meir on the air to teach about Israel; his explanations had such clarity that people loved to listen to him. He would broadcast together with me every year on Tu B'Shvat, Yom HaAtzmaut and Yom Yerushalayim, and he often substituted for me when I went on vacation. When we became a 24-hour network, he created *The Israel Show*, analyzing the Hebrew language and educating listeners on topics they never would have heard about otherwise. His most popular segment was when he played the radio broadcast of the liberation of the Temple Mount in 1967.

Tragically, Meir died suddenly in June of 2021, a loss that affects us until this day. His funeral was standing room only, quite a tribute in our community for a bachelor with very few relatives. The room was filled with people who were direct beneficiaries of Meir's love and friendship, as well as with people who had never met him but felt a closeness as listeners of *JM in the AM*. Unfortunately, due to the strict Covid rules at the time, I was unable to escort Meir to Israel. But, when he arrived in Israel, there were many people at that funeral there as well, demonstrating just how many friends he had on both sides of the ocean.

ZIONISM

To: nachum@wfmu.org
Subject: Yom HaAtzmaut Show

Nachum and Meir,
Yashar kochachem on a great show. Hearing a few more shows like that might provide the final push for us to get up and move La'Aretz.

Thanks.

To: nachum@wfmu.org
Subject: Hatikvah

Boker Tov,

My point today, which my husband and I have made a number of times before, concerns the playing of "Hatikvah" at the end of each program. This is a lovely way to end, but you almost always talk over it. "Hatikvah" is a solemn anthem, not just a song. As an Israeli, my husband feels so strongly about "Hatikvah" that he stands when he hears it, even in our living room while watching something on TV from Israel. It is not something which should be talked over. It's just not appropriate. Hearing this combination jars us every time.

You once said you would consider changing this policy. Won't you please rework the end of your program either by eliminating "Hatikvah" altogether or by playing it with no talking. I don't think that you would consider talking during the playing of "Hatikvah" in Israel, where I know you have been countless times. Give our national anthem, with its timeless plea, the same respect here.

I look forward to your response.

❋ ❋ ❋

To: <Nachum@wfmu.org>
Subject: Yom Yerushalayim

Hi again, Nachum,
Just wanted to tell you that this morning's special Yom Yerushalayim program that you did with Meir Weingarten was GREAT!

It had me crying, smiling, etc., and I understand it had a similar effect on many other people too, judging from conversations I had with folks at Bruriah today.

Incidentally, it also may help push me "over the edge" in terms of a decision regarding sending our son back to KBY for a second year.

❋ ❋ ❋

To: <nachum@wfmu.org>
Subject: Your substitute today in promoting views

Nachum:
You and Meir have certain viewpoints and you feel you must share them with the audience. I found that I did not want to listen to JM in the AM this morning and listen to repeated reasons why we should go to Israel, and listen to the reasons why we should help CAMERA by writing to AP and other places. I do not want to hear sermons in the morning. Stop the sermons. Please.

✻ ✻ ✻

To: nachum@wfmu.org
Subject: Chevron!!!

Dear Nachum,
All the attention and necessary focus that you have placed on the holy city of Chevron has given me this incredible attachment to this wonderful city. Before I left to Israel, I called the Hebron Fund in Brooklyn to find out if there would be any tours going. They gave me Judy Grossman's number in Israel.

We arrived to Israel on Sunday night; on Monday morning I was in touch with Judy and she put me in touch with the tour guide (Rabbi Hochbaum, a real heilige Yid). My wife, son, in-laws, and I registered for a Wednesday tour of Kever Rachel and Chevron. It was unreal!! Wow! An amazing and inspirational tour.

We met with David Wilder; we visited three apartments in Hebron; Ma'arat HaMachpeilah for Mincha; the ancient cemetery; we also got great artwork from the gift shop.

Nachum, thank you for giving us the inspiration to go and experience Hebron. We really felt so safe and holy. Please continue to urge people to visit "the holy city of Hebron."

"Regardless of what you choose to do today — whether you say *Tachanun* or recite *Hallel* — you must take some time to acknowledge the importance of Israel. Recognize that your ability to spend a year learning at the

With Rush Limbaugh at the end of our four day trip to Israel (Summer 1993). My brother, Rabbi Chaim Nate, forged a very close friendship with Rush. It was instrumental in forming his opinion about Israel and The Middle East

Mir, to take a hike in the Golan, or even to sit by the pool at the Inbal is all a result of the fact that Israel exists today."

This mantra, with which I open our annual Yom HaAtzmaut broadcast each year, sums up what I see as my basic role as a Jewish radio personality. I don't try to indoctrinate and I don't try to convert anyone whose position is staunchly opposed to mine. Instead, I try to wake people up to a seemingly simple idea: Israel is the most amazing and important place in the world — and it is ours. In recent years, I have often said on the air what I truly believe: The future of the Jewish people is in the State of Israel.

It is precisely the indifference toward Israel, across the religious and political spectrum, that fuels my unbounded enthusiasm for our homeland, prompting me to spend a relatively large amount of time on the subject. I simply cannot fathom how anyone — especially an individual who enjoys

On Masada w/ (l-r) Meir Weingarten, Malcolm Hoenlein, Rabbi Chaim Nate Segal & Rush Limbaugh (July 1993).

spending Yom Tov at a luxurious Jerusalem hotel, visiting rabbis in Bnei Brak, or bathing in the Dead Sea — can ignore the significance, the magnitude, of our moment in history's timeline. Unquestionably, those activities would be impossible were it not for the founding of the State of Israel, the culmination of a 2,000-year-old dream that our ancestors would have given their right arms to witness.

How did I develop this enthusiasm for Israel and its people? I was raised in a home where Israel was always one of the most important topics discussed. My father's personal history included studying in Hebron in 1929 and knowing many who were killed in that summer's massacre. He also had relationships with prominent leaders in pre-state Israel who would become members of Israel's original and subsequent governments. Once he became a rabbinic leader in the United States, he was involved in shuttle diplomacy that impacted greatly on the establishment and the growth of the State.. In fact, he is given credit for convincing prominent Israeli government officials that women should not be subjected to mandatory national service and that *Sherut Leumi* should be voluntary, prompting the Tchebiner Rav to say that he was jealous of my father's olam haba (share in the next world).

During my year of study at Yeshivat Kerem B'Yavneh, I instantly fell in love with what I saw all around me: Jews walking the streets with confidence and without fear, Jews doing business together, Jews knowing that we are all one family. My passion for Israel only escalated in 1988, when the first intifada erupted. With each visit, first when I was single and then as my family grew, my love for our homeland has only increased.

In 2006, I had the privilege of spending Pesach in Israel for the first time in twenty-five years. It struck me that the ordinary events of everyday life, when experienced in Israel, become extraordinary. Before the holiday began, I took a trip to a Jerusalem mall; it looked like any mall in any country

With Rabbi Chaim Nate Segal meeting Prime Minister Rabin (July 1993).

(l-r) Rush Limbaugh, Rabbi Chaim Nate Segal, Prime Minister Rabin, Malcolm Hoenlein, Nachum (July 1993).

in the world. But at *this* mall I spotted a booth where shoppers could sell their *chametz*.

My listeners are entitled to their opinions, and I realize that the Jewish community is polarized regarding the State of Israel. I find it amusing to get as many phone calls protesting my Zionist programming as those objecting to my tendency to speak during the "Hatikvah" anthem that closes each of our shows. I am likely to receive two emails on the same day, one asking, "How can you display such heresy, playing the anthem of the secular Zionists?" and the other, "How can you show such disrespect, speaking as you broadcast such a holy tune?"

My goal has always been to harness radio's unlimited potential to create a unique bond, one that might otherwise be impossible, between our listeners in America and our brothers and sisters in Israel.

To this end, we dedicate time throughout the year to news from Israel. Each day, we broadcast Jerusalem's weather forecasts. Twice a year, we announce the dates when Israelis change their clocks. During Chol HaMoed Sukkot and Pesach, we alert those who can't be in Israel that they can go online to see *Bircat Kohanim* at the Kotel, the next best thing to being

With (l-r)) David Magence, Rabbi Chaim Nate Segal, Hon Benjamin Netanyahu, Mr and Mrs Chris Lee, Rush Limbaugh & Malcolm Hoenlein (Jerusalem JULY 1993).

there. In these subtle ways, I try to help my listeners feel as if we aren't at least 5,800 miles away from the Holy Land.

We constantly encourage individuals and families to visit Israel. To those planning midwinter, summer, or holiday vacations, we offer this challenge: How can you justify spending all that money to go to Florida or Puerto Rico when you could use it to go to Israel? If you're going on vacation, then vacation in Israel! We suggest that our listeners book as many trips to Israel as possible, as far in advance as they can. Sure, they might cancel a few, but they will surely go on many more trips than they would have by waiting around for what they feel is the ideal time.

During Israel's election seasons, we featured several shows covering their political parties and issues. On both our website and live stream, we presented an election special that clarified matters that even some Israelis find mind-boggling. Our listeners' positive feedback was gratifying; it told us that our programming truly contributed to listeners on both sides of the Atlantic better understanding the election.

With Grand Marshall Robert Ben Rimon at The Celebrate Israel Parade.

Organizations devoted to Israel's welfare are featured on our network. We aim to shed light on the *chesed* activities and political pursuits with which those living in Israel are occupied. Getting Americans involved in these endeavors is important not only from an economic perspective but from a social one as well. We need to truly feel what it is like to live in the Holy Land.

Last but not least, we fill a void by dedicating four shows a year to special days that often pass unnoticed in America: Israel's Memorial Day, Independence Day, Jerusalem Day, and *Tu B'Shvat*. Our objective is to offer listeners a haven for commemorating these days appropriately: with joy, sorrow, or reverence. The time and effort that my volunteer staff and I invest to make these shows come alive cannot be overstated. My good friend and coworker, the late Meir Weingarten, whose influence on my own feelings towards Israel is immeasurable, devoted hours to deciding which special readings and music would produce just the right mood.

With Prime Minister Ariel Sharon & Rabbi Chaim Nate Segal in Samaria.

With Binyamin Segal, Washington 1992.

With Keneset member Rabbi Avraham Ravitz.

Each year, some listeners object to our choice of programming, but most appreciate how our efforts help each of those four days come alive.

On Yom HaAtzmaut and Yom Yerushalayim, most callers greet us with an enthusiastic "Chag Sameach." Many describe how they, in their own

With IDF hero Chanan Porat

small way, are celebrating. Others recall how they spent those days when in Israel. A woman once phoned to say that her children's schools don't acknowledge these holidays, so she thanked us for bringing the spirit of Yom HaAtzmaut into a home that otherwise would have had no way to experience it. Together, we all feel as if we are part of a community *simcha*, as close as possible to being together with our Israeli brothers and sisters.

On all of these days, we purposely play classic songs by Israeli singers, creating nostalgia and, we hope, a yearning to be in Israel. Of course, over the years we've invited special guest speakers to the studio. We share *divrei Torah* about Israel and read appropriate selections from the Prophets. And we always play archival recordings from those historical dates: David Ben-Gurion's reading of the 1948 declaration of independence, and the Israeli army's 1967 liberation of Jerusalem's Temple Mount.

We try to expose listeners to things that are uniquely Israeli. One year we invited Avshalom Kor, an internationally renowned expert on the Hebrew

With 6 Day War Hero General Mordechai Gur.

Nefesh B'Nefesh flight, with Ambassador Danny Danon.

language, to discuss the significance of various Hebrew names. In another year, we broadcast from Israel; what better way to convey the country's festive mood than to capture it on the air? And in yet another, the BBC visited our studio, leading off their Israel Independence Day coverage with a *JM in the AM* clip illustrating how American Jews commemorate Yom HaAtzmaut.

On Tu B'Shvat, we choose to focus on the actual land of Israel. Often, it's one of the most fascinating shows of the year, opening people's minds to ideas and customs they have never heard of before. Once, we broadcasted a Tu B'Shvat *seder* live from the studio and the feedback was enthusiastic beyond description.

For many years we did not dedicate an entire show to Yom HaZikaron (Israel's Memorial Day), but as the demand for it increased, Robert Katz decided to put in the challenging work required to create such a broadcast. We have played appropriate music, recited the names of fallen soldiers,

Celebrate Israel Parade with my lifelong friend, Dr. Richard Friedman OB"M

read excerpts from old Israeli newspaper reports of soldiers' deaths, and described various Israeli Yom HaZikaron ceremonies. Each year, a vast number of listeners call the studio, many close to tears, expressing gratitude for a place to mourn properly, linked with thousands to create the most well-attended Memorial Day event beyond Israel's borders.

On a recent Yom HaZikaron, my brother Yigal described the awesome experience of standing on a Jerusalem corner as the memorial siren sounded. Traffic came to a halt; people froze in their steps. He knew he was being presented with an opportunity to meditate on something profound, but what? Yigal decided to concentrate on the fact that, thanks to those being memorialized, he and his family can walk freely on the streets of Jerusalem. Hearing his words, I could only reply that because of Israeli soldiers who continually risk their lives, we are free to walk the streets of New York. That's how certain I am that the destinies of Israeli and Diaspora Jewry are intertwined.

Miriam L. Wallach with a bunch of t-shirts from the parade route. Miriam exchanges NSN swag for school and group swag all through our parade broadcast.

In May 2007, I visited Jerusalem and Hebron to commemorate — on the air — the fortieth anniversary of the liberation of both holy cities. One of my career's most exhilarating experiences, it left an indelible impression on many listeners. Jerusalem was engulfed by thunderstorms that day, leading many of us to reflect on the heavenly Providence that accompanied that city's liberation. What would have happened, we wondered aloud, had such treacherous weather plagued Israel's army exactly forty years ago?

I believe that with the United States' economic downturn in 2008 there was a strong shift in the relationship between Israel and the Diaspora. With Israel's incredible growth in industry and technology, the Jewish State became significantly less reliant on the Diaspora Jews for support. The tide turned and Israel began to assume the role as the light for Diaspora Jewry.

I think back to so many years of Jewish history when that was not the case,

JM in the AM Tour to Israel

when it was beyond comprehension that Israel would lead such a prominent role. When the rabbis created the calendar of when *parshiyos* are read, they could not have envisioned a time where it would be so incongruent for the Diaspora countries to be behind Israel for so long. Perhaps, had they realized this time would come, there would have been a system in place for the Diaspora countries to catch up more quickly.

Baruch Hashem, so many listeners have told me that, thanks to *JM in the AM*, their positions on Israel have softened and due particularly to our live broadcasts from Israel, they have visited the Holy Land for the first time.

Back in 2004, I received an email I will never forget: "Please wish a *Tzeischem L'Shalom* on your broadcast to the Hebron Mission's contingent from Mt. Kisco Hebrew Congregation. We're leaving this Tuesday night! And thanks again to your program for inspiring this mission. It is without exaggeration to say that, without your inspiration, we would not be going to Hebron."

If even one of those sentences were true, then I am truly blessed to have devoted my life to Jewish radio.

YOU DON'T HAVE TO BE JEWISH

To: Nachum Segal <nachum@wfmu.org>
Subject: Re: thank you VERY much

Nachum,
I appreciate your acknowledgement of my loss immensely, as well as your thoughtful words. It's the kindness of my adopted family at WFMU that helps me (and others here) through good and lean times. I hope for the best for you and your family in return.

I've always appreciated your bonhomie and good humor, and am fondly waiting for the next barrage of chiding from you.

Date: Tue. 27 Mar 2001 08:15:42 EST
Subject: Quick note and thank you

Mr. Segal,

I just wanted to say, someone on the air this morning (Tuesday) mentioned that "You don't have to be Orthodox to enjoy JM in the AM." I'd like to add that you don't have to be Jewish either (I'm not anyway).

I have been listening to your program for quite a few years and it has enlightened me, entertained me and, I'd like to think, improved me as a person. So, to you, and everyone there: THANK YOU!

A very definite fan

To: <Nachum@wfmu.org>

Hello.

I was listening to your show in my car this AM and there was a presentation that interested me. Since I was driving in the snowstorm, I was unable to take any notes on the content, or write down the presenter's name.

A gentleman was explaining about one of three mitzvahs [please pardon my spelling, or misspelling; I am a Catholic!] that a person must perform; and the talk led into a discussion of a parent's obligation to be the primary faith educator for his or her children. Obviously, this is a truism in any religion.

I am involved in religious education at my local church and we are going through a similar process now: reminding parents that while we can provide some education at our church, ultimately the parents are in the best position to be the true educators. Since my faith is founded on Judaism, the sources he cited for this parental responsibility is of interest to me.

Is there any way I can obtain a transcript of this man's talk, or some other way to obtain the content and/or basis of it?

❉ ❉ ❉

The hallways of the small brick building where I worked each morning for over three decades, the home of WFMU, are lined with pictures of obscure musicians and historical figures. The building itself can easily be overlooked amid the towering structures of Jersey City, and the hustle and bustle of mainstream life on the streets contradicts the arcane, unconventional world of freeform radio hosts within its walls. Some days I would walk in to find the night show hosts — in jeans and t-shirts — still sleeping on the couches. On other days I would meet a different group of broadcasting colleagues, many of them trendy, cutting-edge inhabitants of lower Manhattan and its surrounding neighborhoods. Whether in jeans or three-piece suits, their lives were so different from mine — and yet they were my colleagues.

It is from this small shared studio that I woke many inhabitants of the Jewish world, attempting to bring a message of *kedusha* (holiness) into their homes. After so many years, the contradictions within my place of work still astounded me. Still, those contradictions offered me an incredible opportunity: to try and make a daily *Kiddush Hashem* as I interacted with the world beyond my own.

Fortunately for me, this opportunity was one for which I had been prepared all my life. I did not grow up in a big Jewish community where virtually all my neighbors looked and acted exactly like me. As a child, I did not know of a life where all the local stores, parks, and offices catered to the wants and needs of my specific religious community. Instead, I was brought up in a heterogeneous environment, one in which I felt at ease with all kinds of people. I spent my early years in Newark and then Orange, New Jersey. There, my father was the shul rabbi and a highly respected role model to both Jews and non-Jews.

Neither of my parents were born in the United States (my mother was born in Germany; my father in Russia and he moved at age two to what was then called Palestine). Perhaps because of their immigrant status, they fully accepted the friendships my brothers and I cultivated with youngsters unlike us. In fact, my mother, with her characteristically German dignity and charm, would not dream of treating anyone — from our disabled neighbor to our non-Jewish contemporaries — with anything other than the utmost respect. My father always trusted that we'd know our limits, that we could play at our gentile friends' homes without ever eating non-kosher food or behaving inappropriately. This was a trust that my siblings and I greatly appreciated and it helped us become who we are today.

The boys with whom we played most frequently were our Catholic neighbors. My early memories are filled with scenes of us shooting baskets in each other's backyards. Recently, I received an email from one of those childhood friends, after many years without contact. He described how seeds planted during our backyard conversations so long ago had blossomed into an interest in Judaism, leading him to spend a good deal of time in Israel.

For as long as I can remember, my parents always stressed how our words and actions reflect who we are, and how important it is to treat everyone with the utmost respect. But as much as their words hit home, I learned these lessons more profoundly by observing them both in action. I have tried so hard to follow their noble example. A hint that I may have succeeded in some small measure came when someone asked one of my children what he has learned best from his father. He replied, "I learned how to talk to people. I learned that everyone, regardless of their religion, deserves my respect." I feel lucky to have chosen a career and a workplace that enabled me to put these beliefs into practice on a regular basis.

For many Jersey City residents and workers, I may have been the only person wearing a yarmulke they had ever met. I always took care to say good morning to the dozens of people I passed on the way from my car to WFMU's building. Wherever I am working, I try my best to greet all the local business owners with a friendly disposition. Many members of Klal Yisrael share that commitment. Yet, too often, I meet people who feel they are too busy with their own lives, their families, and their insular community to give credence to anyone outside of their inner circle. I feel strongly that this view is wrong and that its consequences are harmful. In contrast, a sincere smile, lasting only a moment, can generate harmony that will last a lifetime.

I cherish the relationships I cultivated with my colleagues at WFMU. From Fabio, the liberal intellectual from the Village, to Bart, with his spiked hair and body piercings, I have gone out of my way to find common ground, focusing on that instead of our differences. If we can chat about sports, music, or politics, if we can just joke around and in that way develop a casual but positive relationship, I believe their perception of Orthodox Jews will be dramatically enhanced.

For a time, I gave rides to some WFMU hosts who, like me, lived in Manhattan. These were people who in all likelihood had never spoken to someone like me before, who might have come from a culture rife with negative images of Orthodox Jews. Still, they felt comfortable approaching me and asking for a ride and I was glad to oblige. In some small way, maybe our shared treks through the Holland Tunnel will make the world a better place.

With Gaylord, one of my colleagues at the radio station, I enjoyed a running joke that lasted a long time. With Stork, a veteran radio host at WFMU, I shared such a strong relationship that when I traveled to Israel with colleagues who otherwise would have replaced me, I was able to ask him to run the technical aspects of *JM in the AM* from the studio while we broadcast from overseas. Of course, these friendships have boundaries of which everyone at the office is well aware. My non-Jewish colleagues knew that I could not go out to eat or drink with them. Still, I think that within the positive context we've built, they see these strong convictions as something to respect rather than abhor.

By going out of my way to discuss their shows and making a point to listen to their opinions, my associates learned to respect my views as well. *JM in the AM* is an island surrounded by an otherwise progressive environment. It is a mouthpiece for the observant Jewish world emanating from a totally non-sectarian place. It espouses right-wing viewpoints about which I would expect to hear much backlash from liberal-thinking colleagues. Instead, I hear words of respect.

Several years ago, Glen Jones, a popular WFMU host, decided he was going to break the Guinness World Record for the longest radio show. He began on Friday night amid a swarm of publicity. After Shabbos, accompanied by my son Binyamin, I headed for the studio to give Glen whatever moral support I could. The praise he showered upon me — going so far as to treat me like a radio icon — and the respect I accorded his venture were not lost on anyone in the studio, including Binyamin. I was so grateful that my son had witnessed what I have tried to teach him all along: respect breeds respect.

I hope that as people read this, they will start to consider the relationships they have with colleagues and acquaintances. And they will understand the importance of incorporating these practices into everyday life. It is important for them as individuals and important for us as a community.

JEWISH RADIO PHENOMENON

To: <nachum@wfmu.org>
Subject: JM in the AM

Dear Nachum,
I've started this email to you ten different ways. In the interest of brevity, here is the short history:

I am the mother of five incredible children. I grew up with 12 years of Catholic school, but gave that up (being Catholic) about six years ago. Since then, I've just been drifting along, which has not felt like the right way to live nor to raise my children. Around that same time, I found out that my birth father (whom I never knew) was Jewish.

In my profession as a midwife, I started serving Orthodox Jewish women and learning about their lives, their traditions, their values, their spirituality. A light inside me was kindled. I wondered what my life would have been like if I had been raised in a Jewish home.

As I was driving to a birth early one morning, I decided to listen to my car radio. I kept turning the dial around but nothing was coming in clearly — until I came to your show. It was during the Three Weeks. My attention was captured by the Rabbi who was speaking. The light that had been kindled inside me began to flicker a little brighter. I found myself listening the next day, and the next. I loved the two-minute morning lessons. It always amazed me how each lesson would come together when at first I could not imagine where it was going. I found myself crying to some of the songs you played, about falling in love in shtetls, about the Holocaust, about the Wall. I found myself listening to music I didn't even understand the words to, but which held me enthralled. I listened to Torah Dimensions tapes, sitting with the car running, even when I had arrived at my destination, because I didn't want to miss the end. Even on days when I didn't have to get up early, I would set my alarm and get up to listen to your show.

By the time Tisha B'Av arrived, I felt like I had prepared for it and decided to fast. I spent the day in prayer, reflecting about where my life was supposed to go. The next night, I woke up at about 4:00 a.m., with the revelation that this was the path I was supposed to be on. In those early morning hours, I saw that with so much clarity. Since then, my kids and I attend shul every Shabbat. We are learning Hebrew, studying with a Rabbi, and are looking forward to conversion.

Here we are again in the Three Weeks. Although it is supposed to be a time of mourning, for me it is a time of inspiration. I wanted to share with you this story of how you helped change the course of my life, my kids' lives, and, hopefully, the lives of many generations to come.

✻ ✻ ✻

To: nachum@wfmu.org
Subject: Hello from a HUGE fan!

Hi there, Nachum. I have been a listener for around 12 years and now …. I am a ripe old 20 years old, so basically I have grown up with you as my wakeup call every morning.

❋❋❋

To: nachum@wfmu.org
Subject: Shlomo Lutsky

I was listening this morning when you mentioned a basketball event. You commented in passing that the coach's name is Shlomo Lutsky. Shlomo is a long-lost cousin of mine!

Can you possibly send me the information about the event so that I might contact him?

Thanks.

❋❋❋

To: nachum@wfmu.org
Subject: question about amputee mentioned on today's show

Hi, Nachum. I am a physiatrist (a physician who specializes in physical medicine and rehabilitation). I wrote to you last year and you mentioned my shul's fundraiser for Steve Averbach, a spinal cord injured victim of terrorism in Israel.

This morning, while driving to work, I heard you mention a groom-to-be who is a recent double lower-extremity amputee. I would like to contact him to see if I can help, but I did not catch the phone number. Could you please send it to me?

❋❋❋

To: ken@wfmu.org
Subject: 90.1 FM

For the past ten months I was incarcerated in the Federal Correctional Facility in Otisville, NY. I am an Orthodox Jew and had the great satisfaction of being able to listen to your JM in the AM program, hosted by Nachum Segal. I cannot tell you enough how the show kept me in tune with events in the Jewish community and gave me "chizuk" to know that one day I would be rejoining civilization. Well, lucky for me that day came last week. Unfortunately, I left behind several friends whose only connection to the outside world is the JM in the AM show.

By the way, let me relate to you a funny story: One morning while I was in prison, I was sitting in the telephone communication center, listening to the radio via my headphones. A repairman working there saw my yarmulke and asked me, "Are you listening to JM in the AM?" I look at him incredulously and asked him to repeat his question. He repeated and explained, "I listen to Nachum every day. I live in Monticello but, because I'm working here today, I can't listen." I felt sorry, because my prison only issued radios operated with headphones. Imagine, even in a desert like Otisville, I met someone else who listens to JM in the AM!

Ken, the purpose of all the above is that I understand that you are considering selling the radio station. I know in these days of bottom-line results, losing propositions are a no-no. However, imagine the public good this radio station is performing when you are literally the lifeline to many Jewish inmates in Otisville, not to mention the telephone guy in Monticello. I have been a contributor to the station in the past and will continue as long as you continue to offer fine Jewish programming like JM in the AM. You seem to have a good Jewish heart (from the few times I have heard you on the show), so I hope you will keep Nachum on the air for our friends Upstate.

When I first began my career in radio, I didn't have any great vision of its potential or any notion of its tremendous possibilities. I just knew it was something I loved and something I wanted to be a part of. The more I became involved, however, the more I realized the universal language with which radio communicates and the countless ways in which people's lives are enriched by it. During my first few years of broadcasting, I realized that we were on the road to accomplishing this goal but I also understood that it would take time to get there.

With the passage of time, *baruch Hashem*, the show gained more listeners, more impact, and more credibility. Still, there are people who ask questions like "Why do you devote so much time to your show?" or "What about your listener-supported show makes it worthy of my charity dollars?" Even some of my most loyal listeners ask questions like "What about *JM in the AM* justifies your decision to forgo davening Shacharis with a minyan?" or "Why have you relinquished the possibility of earning more money?"

The following anecdotes — selected from hundreds of others — will, I hope, answer these questions and, in the process, illustrate this incredible phenomenon known as Jewish radio. Its success is a result of a powerful medium, an extraordinarily receptive audience, and the hard work of so many people. It has been my good fortune to be at the center of Jewish radio, watching it

Live on air with my devoted Chief Engineer ZK (Zalman Kopel) and the all important Sushi Platter.

Nachum w/ Larry Wachsman, Jerusalem May 1989. Yes, we actually did a live show from a cordless phone. Larry is one of the handful of people who are actually responsible for my career.

grow into something resembling a mix between a yeshiva, a *kiruv* organization, and, above all, the most inclusive Jewish community. It is, I believe, the greatest story never told, one whose time has finally come.

Two very different stories illustrate the wide-ranging appeal of the show: from a person lacking Jewish prestige to a tremendous *talmid chacham*. My older brother Nate was driving in Staten Island one Friday, enjoying Rabbi Yudin's weekly Torah portion broadcast. When he reached his destination, he parked his car and started walking toward his destination. Strangely, he kept hearing the *derasha* and could not figure out how that was possible. Suddenly, he noticed a homeless man in tattered clothes on his right, pushing a shopping cart containing all his earthly possessions. In it was a radio from which he was listening raptly to Rabbi Yudin's Torah thoughts.

Broadcasting from Davidman's Homowack. Lots of CD's, lots of machines. Very 1990's.

In contrast, my neighbor was speaking recently to a highly respected rosh yeshiva and was trying to remember the time of day that a particular event occurred. Suddenly, the rosh yeshiva exclaimed, "I remember! It was around eight o'clock at night, right after Randi Wartelsky's news update on the 'Nachum Segal Show.'"

One morning during a fundraising marathon, we announced two pledges in a row. The first was from a woman in Brooklyn, acknowledging the great music she hears each morning and pledging a donation in honor of her son's *upsherin*. The second was from a woman in Poughkeepsie, thanking the show for giving her family a meaningful connection to Judaism and pledging a donation in honor of her daughter's forthcoming bat mitzvah party at her local temple. This was certainly an interesting contrast.

Immediately following 2004's tragic tsunami in the Indian Ocean, Mattes Weingast, my staff member with the most seniority, called Thailand's Chabad rabbi to learn how we could support the relief effort. When Mattes introduced himself, the rabbi immediately asked, to Mattes's surprise, "Mattes, why weren't you on the air this morning?" So far from home, the rabbi and his family considered the show their connection to New York's vibrant Jewish life. Even in the midst of their crisis, they continued to listen.

A leader in the Reform movement once sent us an email that I'll never forget. He wrote, "I enjoy the content of your program, but I especially want to congratulate you on a format which is, while obviously of traditional orientation, just as obviously thoroughly all-embracing. This is an attitude all too rare today."

Proud Listener

With Dr. Marc Singer, The man known as Film Guy to my listeners, and Binyamin Segal

Several more gratifying stories underscore how integral the show has become to so many. An email we received after a staff trip to Israel spoke volumes about the warm sense of community that the show has engendered over the years. We had been planning the trip for some time and had been discussing it excitedly on the air. It would be Mattes's first trip to Israel and the first time our team of six would be traveling together. Our plan, enthusiastically described to the listeners in the preceding weeks, was to broadcast from Israel, describe what we were doing and especially to depict what it was like to see the Holy Land through Mattes's eyes. Upon our return, we received this email: "When I heard on the air that you had arrived in Israel, I had goosebumps all over. I had to pull the car over; I was so moved that I was crying."

A listener from New Jersey told me that when he heard the news on the radio that my wife, Staci, had given birth to triplets, he was so excited that he ran to the nearest payphone to call his wife. As he waited impatiently outside the occupied phone booth, he overheard the animated conversation coming from within: "Guess what I just heard? Nachum and Staci Segal had triplets this morning!"

Jumbo Sept. 2000 NYT article

Ruchie Robinson, a loyal listener, had this to say in a *New York Times* feature published on September 24, 2000: "I can't have a baby or celebrate a birthday without Nachum. If it's not on *JM in the AM*, it didn't happen." Mayer Fertig, a member of my team who often sits in for me, asserts that he prefers to host the show on Friday because "I feel like I've really made it in the world when Rabbi Yudin says, 'Good morning, Mayer.'" A doctor who was on a medical mission in Zimbabwe wrote that he stayed connected by listening to *JM in the AM* every Friday.

Still, for me, the most incredible part of the phenomenon is the show's ability to unite otherwise disparate (and occasionally argumentative) segments of the Jewish community. There is a chassid from Brooklyn with whom I would never have crossed paths; our families are different, our communities are

Listeners over the years have sent us photos of JM in the AM merch in interesting places. Bottom left: two fans (The Speisers) at The Great Wall of China sporting their JM tees.

different, and even our ideas about religion are worlds apart. Still, he has become an avid listener to both *JM in the AM* and the Nachum Segal Network. Last year, when he pledged money during the marathon, he explained that the shows present millions of opinions with which he disagrees. Yet, not only does he enjoy the shows, he also holds them in high regard for creating an atmosphere devoid of dissent and negative language, for managing to create quality programming without ever spouting *lashon hara* about any member or segment of the Jewish community.

One morning, a listener called from Eugene, Oregon, describing the community's desperate need for a *Sefer Torah*. Moved by the plea along with the intervention of Rabbi Nate Segal, a devoted New York listener, Leon Goldenberg, donated a Torah and flew out to Oregon to take part in the *hachnasat Sefer Torah.* "Imagine!" he told me. "There I was in a place that, before this adventure, I never would have been able to locate on a map!"

The shows' extraordinary ability to unite also generates an unprecedented ability to serve. *Baruch Hashem*, in innumerable ways, *JM in the AM* has come through for diverse members of the Jewish community. During the summer blackout of 2003, I was driving from an appointment in Baltimore to New York in the pre-dawn hours of Friday, August 15, and blissfully unaware of what people in the Northeast were facing, I opted to go straight to the morning show studio instead of stopping at home. Incredibly, WFMU's headquarters was the only building on the block that had electricity, a fact many attributed to good luck and I, of course, credited to the One Above. We used our good fortune to let the public know which Jewish communities had electricity and where people could go on that Erev Shabbos if they were stranded. The Jewish community's incredible generosity shone that morning as countless listeners called the studio to extend Shabbos invitations to total strangers.

Similarly, when a 1999 strike brought Ben Gurion Airport to a standstill just before Sukkot, one of Israel's busiest tourist seasons, thousands of our listeners were distraught. To the rescue came Munich's Chabad rabbi. One week before Yom Tov, he called the studio. "If the strike isn't resolved before Yom Tov and you're stranded in Europe en route to Israel," he told our audience, "here are your options for spending Sukkot in Europe." *Mi k'amcha Yisrael!*

As the turn of the century approached, we began an on-air discussion about who was the most important Jew of the 20th century. Many people sent in suggestions such as the Lubavitcher Rebbe or the IDF soldier. Eventually I invited Jewish historian Dr Jeffrey Gurock to give his opinion and to discuss the topic with our audience.

September 11, 2001, 9:00 a.m. I had just finished the morning show when WFMU staffer Kelly Jones called to report that a plane had just crashed into the World Trade Center. Shaken, we all rushed outside. From our Jersey City studio, we gazed across the Hudson River, watching in horror as the Twin Towers fell. We had a direct view of the billowing black smoke; of the tragic collapse of the buildings; of ambulances speeding through the Holland Tunnel to treat the injured; and of survivors rushing to the PATH station, desperate to flee Manhattan. Like all Americans, we were numb with grief. But we knew it was our responsibility to broadcast a Jewish perspective on the tragedy. I slept at the station that night, knowing that it would be impossible to make it home and back again for the next day's show. As difficult as it was, we put together a radio response to the catastrophe in less than 24 hours. We recited *Tehillim*, interviewed Twin Towers survivors, and, along with our listeners, gained *chizuk* from Rabbi Goldwasser's insights into finding faith in times of crisis.

Many listeners, reaching us later that day by phone or email, expressed astonishment that we had been able to broadcast at all. Even when a crisis is comparatively tiny — say, a record-breaking blizzard — many callers are amazed that we actually made it to the studio. As someone who has built his career on a commitment to live radio, I can only reply, "How could we *not* make it to the studio? And, of course, the show must go on."

My commitment to live radio, however, doesn't hold a candle to my listeners' commitment to Torah. A woman emailed us last year with gratifying news: With her help, her daughter had finished learning all the books of *Nach*, the Biblical Prophets, in honor of her upcoming bat mitzvah. And, amazingly, she insisted that *JM in the AM* deserved the credit! Their daunting project took root when mother and daughter had heard one of our inspiring guests bemoaning the fact that too few people study *Nach*. The entire *JM in the AM* team was genuinely moved to learn that our modest show had generated a commitment to, and love for, Torah study.

Another listener's correspondence brought tears to our eyes. "Although we are Jewish, my husband and I never learned all the ins-and-outs of our tradition. That is why, until now, my husband has lit yahrzeit candles for his deceased parents on the secular anniversaries of their passing; perhaps we're ignorant, but we do make an effort. In the future, we'll try to be more conscious of using the lunar calendar. Thanks for educating us."

If I had to choose one favorite illustration of the show's ability to educate, this is it: Two young merchant marines, Jewish by birth but deprived of a Torah education, saw a *JM in the AM* magnet on their host's refrigerator door. Curious, and perhaps a little bored at their post, they began to listen to our show. They were immediately captivated by the clarity and warmth of Rabbi Goldwasser's daily features. Each week, they found themselves purchasing books to delve further into the broadcasts. Gradually, the two young men decided to become Torah observant — all because of Rabbi Goldwasser's sincere and lucid contributions to *JM in the AM*.

Deeply moved, I invited these two *baalei teshuva* to join me on the air. On the morning of their interview, I arrived at the studio at my regular time, 5:30 a.m. And there, on WFMU's front lawn, stood two merchant marines in full uniform — and *tefillin*. I will never forget that sight as long as I live. Years later, I encountered one of them while on vacation and had the pleasure of meeting his wife and first child.

We all know that throughout life's interactions, a small gesture can have huge repercussions. In the invisible medium of radio, there are no gestures. There are only words and voices. I've learned from my listeners that a single word, a brief sentence, an in-depth interview, a caring voice, or even a vocal inflection can — and does — have huge repercussions. I pray that the words and voices emanating from our studios reverberate On High, helping in some small way to bring our ultimate Redemption.

PROMOTING CAUSES

To: nachum@wfmu.org, nachum@jmintheam.org
Subject: Re: FD

Nachum:
Hi there! Hope all is well with you and yours. I was listening with great interest to your show this morning. I was recently contacted by a doctor in North Carolina who is looking for info on the disorder you discussed with David Stein this morning. She has a child with it. If you would be good enough to send her a tape of today's show with contact info for David Stein, I'm sure she would be grateful.

B'hatzlacha

✻ ✻ ✻

To: nachum@wfmu.org
Subject: Thank You.

Nachum — Awesome interview this morning with Rabbi Schacter. Rave reviews.... I really appreciate it; we got so many calls already regarding the tour.

Perhaps you'll find the time to join us on one of these tours....

❋ ❋ ❋

To: Nachum@wfmu.org
Subject: (no subject)

I want to thank you for announcing the Bronx Jewish Community Council's request for a sukkah for a Bronx hospice. We received six calls — four of them from your program's announcement. I am thrilled to report to you that we not only bought a new sukkah for the hospice with donations from your listeners, but we also placed three other recycled sukkot and received two extremely generous cash donations for our emergency fund from your listeners.

We cannot thank you enough for supporting this very worthy cause and for supporting the Jewish communities of the Bronx. In a time of such difficult news, it is so heartwarming to know that someone wants to really make a difference. The other sukkot, the recycled ones, went to a synagogue and to an assisted living nursing home. We cannot thank you enough!

❋ ❋ ❋

Subject: Belated thank you.
To: nachum@wfmu.org

Dear Nachum,

About three years ago, a very close friend's son (four years old) had a relapse after a bone marrow transplant. My calls to your show were constant, asking you to announce his name so people would daven for him. In numerous shuls, his name was on Tehillim lists, but throughout the area people were saying that they already had his name from JM in the AM.

There were public shiurim for his refuah. You announced them. Many of us donated to your marathon with the dedication earmarked as a refuah shleimah for him.

Baruch Hashem, Rafael is doing well, at age 7, after a second transplant, bli ayin hara. May Hashem continue to give him and his family only good things!

The reason I am writing this to you is that for many years when you announce the names of people to daven for, I write the names down and daven for them. Thank you. Thank you. Thank you for giving hope to families like you did to the family of Rafael Shmuel Avraham ben Rochel Leah. Thank you for giving the rest of us the opportunity to participate in this mitzvah. Together with your announcements and the people who react, we accomplish tefillas rabbim, and in this case, it helped!

To: nachum@wfmu.org

Dear Nachum,
I have to give you a Yasher Koach. During the past few months, we have had several volunteers come to Livnot U'Lehibanot who mentioned that they first heard about us on your show. However, there is one story I need to tell you:

Early in May, someone from Englewood heard about the Livnot volunteer project to help out during the current matzav from your show. He decided to come with his son, who was then a senior at Ramaz. They came for about two weeks and really did a lot of volunteer work: painting, serving food in soup kitchens, packing meals for needy families, etc. The New Jersey Jewish Times did a feature story about him and his son, and other people in the community heard about it. Now, a group of about fifteen women from Englewood are coming to do volunteer work at Livnot because of the experience of that father and son — and it all started with your show. The women will be here during the week of October 19th, and I would be happy to arrange for you to interview them (at our expense) so they can describe their volunteer work in Israel.

❋ ❋ ❋

At the start of my broadcasting career at WFMU — about ten days into it, to be exact — my general manager Bruce Longstreet approached me with what seemed like a pretty innocuous idea: "I was thinking that maybe we could veer away from the usual Jewish broadcasting formula that includes only Jewish music and try to enhance the show by combining music with discussions of Jewish issues." With that, Bruce walked off. But, what developed as a result of his suggestion even he could not possibly have imagined.

As a twenty-year-old starting out in the business, I had ideas about Jewish radio. I wanted to eliminate the notion that Jewish radio is only for older people. I had some thoughts on bringing in elements from my college show to make Jewish radio more appealing to younger members of the community. And, I figured it might be a good idea to invite some individuals to discuss various issues on the air. But it soon dawned on me that my show could do more than that: It could play a crucial role in educating my listeners, sensitizing them to causes that otherwise would have remained completely foreign to them or that they would have purposely avoided. In more recent years, with the popularity of social media and the explosion in methods of disseminating information, it might be asked what unique role we play. I see my role as remaining important in two ways: I try to choose causes that are not always so well-known on other platforms, and I promote those causes which I feel are important with extra passion and enthusiasm. Listeners have told me that they turn to us to know what they should be thinking about.

When Amudim was starting to expand, they wanted to be interviewed to enhance their fundraising capabilities. A highly respected rabbi told them that they should be interviewed only on a show like ours because we act responsibly and ask the right questions about sensitive community issues.

I've seen the successes of our campaigns both financially and otherwise. One organization that I speak about often is Otsar. As a result, a listener got involved because he was inspired by what we had spoken about on the air and eventually he became president of the organization. There are elderly sisters who listen from New Jersey every morning who have told us that they send checks to any organization that we promote. Ohr Meir U'bracha, Nefesh B'Nefesh, and FIDF are organizations connected to Israel that are very familiar to our listeners because we speak about them often. I like to highlight Bris Avrohom, Achiezer, and Hatzalah's Chevra Gemach because I see them as some of the unique causes that make a real difference. I know they are not wasting a penny and I like to bring them *chizuk* by announcing their efforts on the air.

I've seen over the years that you never know what is going to inspire someone to donate money or to become involved, as different messages speak to different people. Among the causes that I have highlighted over the years are Hebron, Ohel, Sharsheret, Crib Efrat, and so many more.

Hebron

For many years, the mere mention of the city of Hebron would evoke in most people images of radical settlers and exceedingly dangerous living conditions. Nobody except a staunch right-wing fundamentalist, said the prevailing conventional wisdom, would ever approach the place. But I had always had a completely different view of this holy city. That's why I considered it crucial to convey a personal side of the city, to show my listeners that there are real people living in Hebron — men, women, and children — who simply want to live, work, and play like the rest of us.

So, on the Monday morning following the November 2002 Friday-night massacre in Hebron, in which twelve Israelis had been murdered by Arab terrorists, I announced on the air that I would be leaving that afternoon to visit the families who had lost loved ones. I landed on Tuesday and went directly to visit the families. I presented my Tuesday-morning broadcast of

My get together w/ Rabbi Avi Weiss and Rav Shlomo Levinger days after the 2002 Hebron massacre. Two believers in resistance and demonstrations. I remember how Rabbi Weiss observed how he never spent one night in prison in Israel and Rav Levinger stated how he never spent a night in jail outside of Israel.

JM in the AM from Hebron, walking around the city and describing the aspects of everyday Jewish life that flourish there. For a significant period, I stood outside the local gift shop, urging listeners to make purchases online and support the businesses that were failing as a result of the Arab intifada.

By Wednesday morning, I was back in my New Jersey studio, but the message of that trip is still reverberating to this day. Immediately after the trip, I received emails from five people, including a prominent Orthodox rabbi, who said that my trip had inspired them to visit Hebron as well. In the following weeks, the Hebron gift shop's website became significantly busier, which the owners attributed to the show's enthusiastic promotion. But even more importantly, my trip allowed more people to see Hebron in a positive light, to talk about the city more openly in mainstream conversations, and to feel a more personal connection to its inhabitants. During subsequent visits to Hebron, American teenagers have offered me thanks simply because their parents permitted them to be there only after hearing that I was a frequent visitor. I know parents do not think that my presence ensures their child's physical safety, but I guess they feel less anxious after realizing that visiting Hebron is a normal, acceptable thing to do.

Ohel

In 1988, I received a desperate phone call from the office of Ohel Children's Home and Family Services. An inordinate number of children needed foster homes, but not enough families were willing to take them in. We decided to move into action without delay, knowing that our unique medium would enable us to make a real difference.

The following day, we devoted an entire show to Ohel. We interviewed present and past foster parents about the challenges and joys of foster parenthood. We interviewed Ohel administrators about the severe shortage of Jewish foster parents and what our community could do about it. Our goal was simply to get the message out that foster parenting is not just for the saintly few but for average people armed with commitment and compassion.

Ohel's representatives told our listeners that one of the organization's biggest obstacles was the fear of failure most people felt when they considered taking in a foster child. We wanted our broadcast to obliterate that fear. Apparently, thank G-d, the show was successful, because foster homes were miraculously found and an emergency was averted. Ever since, Ohel representatives have been our frequent guests, keeping the community aware of their important work, dispelling misconceptions about foster care — not to mention Ohel's other important services — and helping us all to make a difference in ways big or small.

Sharsheret

To keep the show interesting and to offer airtime to as many individuals as possible, we rarely invite a guest to present the same topic more than once. In October 2005, Rochelle Shoretz *a"h* of Sharsheret, an organization serving young Jewish women living with breast cancer, convinced me that it was important for her to return to the show.

During subsequent interviews, she said about being on the air, "I want to thank you for being a true partner in this endeavor. Every year after we come on the show, we get calls immediately afterward, and then in subsequent days, from women who have started doing self-exams or have begun using the resources of our organization. You are really saving lives." I feel privileged to have been on Rochelle's team and to know that Jewish women, once suffering with no clue that Sharsheret existed, are now aware of its services because of our broadcasts.

When I think about the number and variety of organizations that have benefited from being on our show, I am truly astounded. Scores of their representatives tell me they've raised more money and have had significantly more people at their annual dinners, because of the airtime offered by our show. Urgent matters long considered taboo, such as spousal abuse, infertility, and Attention Deficit Disorder, were offered a long-overdue public forum over our airwaves. My colleagues and I feel privileged to have helped shatter the silence under which those subjects had been buried.

Crib Efrat

Sometimes, we will feature a topic that is new to virtually all listeners, no matter where they stand on our community's religious and political spectrum. Dr. Theo Sussheim *a"h* was executive director of Crib Efrat, an organization that defrays medical and childcare costs for women who agree to carry their unborn baby to term instead of aborting. In bringing Dr. Schussheim to the studio, we publicized Judaism's reverence for life and childbirth, a foreign notion for many of our non-Orthodox listeners. Conversely, Dr. Schussheim's presence shone a spotlight on a topic of great interest to the general Jewish population but rarely discussed in Orthodox circles: abortion.

Publicizing the needs and missions of major organizations is only a tiny fraction of what the show does for the Jewish community. Because we reach such a large and diverse audience, we have an exclusive — and inclusive — opportunity to expose people to speakers and ideas they would otherwise never hear. Dr. Ari Greenspan has shed light on topics about which most of us, regardless of religious affiliation, would have to plead ignorance: the kosher status of certain exotic fish, various customs for baking matzah, the oral tradition about the kashrut of specific birds, and the history of various types of *esrogim*. All are fascinating subjects that would have a very slim chance of reaching the masses were it not for *JM in the AM*.

For some listeners, the only opportunity they will ever have to hear the stories of world-renowned speakers like Rabbi Paysach Krohn or Rabbi Dovid Goldwasser is on our show. Many have written to tell us they never dreamed they would learn *Mishnayos*, let alone any other Jewish text. But for years they tuned into Rabbi Goldwasser's nightly learning spot and, as a result, felt proud to have learned so much and so consistently. Many others, normally surrounded by political correctness, tell us they never hear representatives of Israel's religious Zionist communities express their ideas and ideals — except over our airwaves.

Looking back on my broadcasting career, I'm amazed by how much my colleagues and I underestimated the role our show would play in the Jewish community. With the passing of each of the last forty years, the awesome responsibility I feel for my listeners keeps growing. Regarding those for whom our show is their only connection to Judaism, I keep asking myself what more I can do to expose them to the beauty of our heritage. And regarding those for whom our show is just a small part of their actively Jewish lives, I'm always wondering what new cause or guest can inspire them.

We have always made the effort to promote causes that are not necessarily in need of financial support but have other needs as well. Radio offers an opportunity, unlike a print ad, to explain, inspire, and answer questions. We have been strongly encouraging listeners to get involved in Partners in Torah. Someone recently approached me and shared that he has had the same Partners in Torah learning partner for thirteen years because *JM in the AM* convinced him to start.

Following Hurricane Sandy and the damage it caused to many Long Island homes, we broadcast live from the Young Israel of Woodmere and spoke to many people in challenging situations. We highlighted the causes to support, especially Achiezer, and informed people as to where they could donate clothing.

In the Spring of 2023, on the morning that Joey Borgen's attackers were appearing before the judge, we persuaded many listeners to go to the courthouse to show support for Borgen. We have been honored to serve as a

Sukkah Shadchan, matching up many owners of *sukkahs* no longer needed with others in need of *sukkahs*. During the blackout of 2003, many were left without power while others who had power were willing to donate their extra freezer space. We were the information center that people accessed if they had a need or wanted to help. During the Y2K scare, when people were worried about what would happen to computer systems when the calendar switched to the year 2000 at midnight on Friday night, we invited Hatzalah members onto the show to share the precautions people should take before Shabbos.

Yanky Meyer would come on the show every summer to discuss Catskills safety precautions. He would explain how to react if listeners encountered a bear, where construction was taking place, and pool safety rules. Even in the social media age, when listeners could have gotten this information elsewhere, many preferred to hear it from him on the show, as he explained it so clearly.

We have brought to listeners' attention the organization Achi that encourages people to "Think Israel – Buy Israeli." They promote making significant changes in buying habits by choosing Israeli products of all kinds. They created a unique concept of displaying these products in a specifically dedicated *klee* (vessel) that functions as a constant reminder of our connection to Israel and its people.

During the Covid pandemic, we never missed a show, understanding our essential role in helping people maintain a sense of community. We promoted social distancing and, eventually, the vaccine and the need to begin returning to regular life. We followed the Israel travel story closely to share with our listeners, and we initiated an employment matching program to help those who had lost their jobs during the pandemic.

One of my regular guests, Malcolm Hoenlein, executive vice chairman of the Conference of Presidents of Major American Jewish Organizations, knows firsthand how receptive our audience is. With such a prominent position, he is invited to speak at many prestigious gatherings and on shows reaching significantly more listeners than ours. Yet, he chooses to spend half an hour each week addressing the *JM in the AM* audience. "I get more reaction from my appearances on *JM in the AM* than I do from CNN," Mr. Hoenlein told the *New York Times*. "Nachum has a committed audience, more oriented to the issues I discuss. People remember what you say on the program. It's an unusual phenomenon."

I am gratified that Mr. Hoenlein's assessment is shared by many. We now get hundreds of calls from people wanting to harness radio to further their cause and reach as many people as possible. Unfortunately, time constraints make it impossible to host them all, and it's difficult to decide which to host. Still, we try to showcase as many causes as possible, even if only for a few minutes. Above all, we do our best to captivate our exceedingly diverse listeners, constantly evaluating how we can contribute most effectively to each segment of that audience.

POLITICAL INVOLVEMENT

Subject: Kol hakovod!
To: nachum@wfmu.org

Nachum:
A major kol hakovod for helping to make Sunday's rally at Dag Hammarskjöld Plaza a success (covered by WINS, WCBS, the New York Post, the Associated Press, NYNews, Channels 1, 2, 4, 5, 7, 9, 11, Israel TV and more).

Subject: Welcome back
To: nachum@wfmu.org

Good morning, Nachum. Welcome back to the States. It was nice to hear your voice this morning. Your segment with Assemblyman Dov Hikind was an extremely moving part of the program. His emotions spoke louder than words. I spoke with a few people about it and we all were very moved.

After discussions with many participants, I realized that you helped many people overcome a powerful post-9/11 fear of joining large, pro-Israel gatherings. May we never have to assemble for such a purpose again.

As time went by and our show's audience grew exponentially, it became clear that a valuable way to capitalize on the show's growth would be in the political arena. We used our medium to encourage listeners to become involved through voter registration drives, rallies for Israel, protest demonstrations, contacting public officials, and letter writing campaigns. In the late summer of 1993, the lucky beneficiaries of our captive audience were political candidates who wanted to attract Jewish voters.

It was during the tight mayoral race between Rudolph Giuliani and David Dinkins that the show began to offer a significant political public service. Recognizing that the Jewish vote could sway the election, Giuliani asked us for air time. We were more than happy to grant it. After all, Mayor Dinkins had made questionable, even biased, judgment calls against New York City's Jewish population. When Giuliani won the election by a margin of merely 50,000 votes, he attributed part of that victory to getting his message out to *JM in the AM* listeners.

MC'ing at Gracie Mansion w/ Mayor Rudy Giuliani, PM Bibi Netanyahu, Dore Gold and others. (1998)

During Giuliani's eight years in office, our relationship grew stronger. I am particularly grateful for my even-closer friendship with his chief of staff, Bruce Teitelbaum. I was invited four times to Gracie Mansion to MC events — notably the Holocaust Museum dedication — and to MC the first Town Hall meeting after Giuliani's election. He could easily have chosen a prominent rabbi or wealthy campaign contributor; being selected was truly an honor. Giuliani continued to be interviewed on the show. In fact, his first public statement after daringly evicting Yasser Arafat from Lincoln Center was made the next morning on *JM in the AM*. I felt privileged to be able to thank him publicly on behalf of the Jewish community.

In November 1994, during the Cuomo/Pataki gubernatorial race, our political involvement got serious — serious enough that both the *New York Post* and the *Daily News* reported that New York State politicians were

Pinny Ringel, Sen Simcha Felder, Assemblyman Dov Hikind, Nachum (The Regency, Brooklyn). The three of them are among many government officials who have been very helpful to me and who have taken great pride in the work and accomplishments of JM in the AM.

"running after Nachum Segal's mike." If these words were a feather in anybody's cap, they undoubtedly were directed at the astute *JM in the AM* audience. Nevertheless, it was thrilling to play a part in this animated political contest.

Not only was the race tight but, to top it off, the Jewish vote was split down the middle. Each candidate had to secure as many Jewish votes as he possibly could. To that end, both Cuomo and Pataki, or their representatives, were featured on the show almost daily. Each was given the time to express his views and make his best attempt to win the Jewish vote. As Election Day drew closer, the suspense in the studio mounted dramatically. It was one of the most riveting periods of my broadcasting career.

Over the years, I've received complaints from both ends of the spectrum: listeners who feel we devote too much time to politics and those who clamor for more. In attempting to maintain a healthy balance, we have never reverted to the Cuomo/Pataki campaign experience, during which we heard from politicians every day. Yes, it was fun, even thrilling, but I can see how it could get tedious after a while. Still, I do feel that it's important to maintain *JM in the AM*'s status as the medium through which local — and not so local — politicians can reach the Jewish community.

To that end, we continue to maintain a close relationship with several local government officials. The late New York State Assembly Speaker Sheldon Silver addressed our audience many times. Two of our most entertaining shows took place in Albany, where we were hosted by the Speaker. In 1999,

Hosting Simcha Felder NY City Council Inauguration. Simcha is an incredible friend. The Jewish community is lucky to have him in a government leadership role.

Mr. Silver invited the entire New York State Legislature to a lunch reception for the expressed purpose of allowing its members to meet us. He considered it important for them to view *JM in the AM* as a conduit to their Jewish constituents.

Many government officials frequent *JM in the AM*. They include former Brooklyn Borough President Marty Markowitz, former NY State Assemblyman Dov Hikind, NY State Assemblywoman Nily Rozic, and NY State Governor Kathy Hochul. They have addressed pressing community issues on our airwaves. While David Greenfield was NYC Councilman, he had a weekly spot on the show and became very close to me, my family, and my listeners.

I know our listeners, as well as our elected officials, appreciate our studio's relaxed atmosphere. And for many years we instituted a weekly spot, "The Felder Focus" on the Nachum Segal Show, during which Simcha Felder, then a councilman, now a state senator who serves a large segment of our listening audience, had the opportunity to update our listeners on the goings-on in his largely Jewish district. It was, in fact, Simcha Felder who was responsible for my close relationship with Mayor Bloomberg.

When he was elected in 2001, New York City Mayor Michael Bloomberg became our frequent guest. He even honored us with his presence, live in the studio, during the annual *JM in the AM* fundraising marathon. During his successful bid for reelection, he frequently used the show to reach the greatest number of Jewish voters. We were happy to oblige. On one unique show, we broadcasted live from the mayor's newly established Boro Park campaign office.

Perhaps my most thrilling interactions with Mayor Bloomberg have taken place off the air. His Honor invited me to join him and then Jerusalem

With Mayor Ed Koch at Gracie Mansion. Will never forget how he honored my request to come over to my mother (a stroke victim like him) and say hello. They spoke about old time Newark and she told him how much she always liked him.

Mayor Uri Lopolianski for dinner. An even greater honor occurred in March 2004, when he invited me to accompany him to Israel, where we represented the United States at the Yad Vashem dedication. Beginning with the delegation flight in Mayor Bloomberg's private plane, the trip was unforgettable. When we reached Jerusalem, we were part of a full-city lockdown that made way for our motorcade's safe arrival. At mealtime, we sat around talking about politics, business, and even sports. Most of all, being part of the United States delegation to Yad Vashem was truly a once-in-a-lifetime event. It wouldn't have happened were it not for the respect Mayor Bloomberg accorded our listeners.

I have also been very lucky to meet and interact with prominent politicians. In 1996, my good friend, the late Councilman and Judge Noach

With President Clinton

Dear took me to meet President Bill Clinton and Vice President Al Gore. I was introduced to the president as the Jewish world's most influential radio host and then the President asked me, after seeing my height, if I play basketball. I told him that I am asked that all the time, but did not expect to be asked by a United States president. I was invited to the White House when George W. Bush was president. While standing in line, I could not decide what I should say to him. Finally, I decided to use the opportunity to thank him for all that he has done for Israel and the Jewish people.

The late, great, Judge Noach Dear deserves additional recognition. There was no government official in the first forty years of my career who took interest, exuded pride, and demonstrated concern for my efforts like he did. He acted as an older brother to me with love, guidance, and creativity. He is missed every day.

With Malcolm Hoenlein & President Clinton.

With VP Al Gore and Hon Noach Dear.

134 | POLITICAL INVOLVEMENT

With Senator Bob Dole.

With NJ Congressman Donald Payne.

With VP Candidate Jack Kemp.

The show's responsibility to the public does not end with local government affairs. We also try to serve as a conduit through which Israel's government officials can reach our community. Geographically distant but emotionally close, we are grateful that *JM in the AM* bridges the cultural, geographic, and linguistic differences between Israeli and American Jewry, allowing an easier exchange of ideas.

On one occasion, then Prime Minister Ehud Olmert invited us to broadcast live from his office, realizing that it would be the best way to convey his ideas to the American public. We've hosted several Knesset members over the years, and even Ariel Sharon and Bibi Netanyahu have been given their requested airtime. In fact, community activist Dr. Joe Frager once told Netanyahu, certainly in jest, "If you want to get elected, you have to go on the Nachum Segal Show."

As hard as it is to decide how much airtime to devote to politics, I think virtually everyone can appreciate the important role that the show has played in this arena. People often ask, "How do you choose which politicians to feature on your show?" The answer is that I'll grant airtime to any politicians who ask for it, as long as their message matters to our community. If we can leverage the influence of our tens of thousands of listeners, Jews who represent our community's broad religious and cultural spectrum, then we have used our airwaves wisely. And that — more than private jets and invitations to Gracie Mansion — is what we have set out to do.

POSITIVE PROGRAMMING

To: Nachum@wfmu.org
Subject: you are the best

I listen to you every morning on the way to Yeshiva in Staten Island. I catch the 8:00 hour. YOU ARE MAMESH THE BEST.

You put me in such a "heimishe" mood that the second that I walk into shiur, I get right into it. You get part of the "s'char" for my limudim.

KEEP UP THE AWESOME WORK.

A MAJOR JM IN THE AM FAN!!!

❈ ❈ ❈

To: nachum@wfmu.org
Subject: thanx for a great job...

Nachum Segal,
I just wanted to say kol hakavod for all the great music that you play every morning (and at night). I listen to JM in the AM while going to school and it is just great. I am in a secular university, so to hear Jewish music every morning before I get to school is a breath of fresh air, it makes my day better, and it reminds me of my Jewishness before entering a very non-Jewish place.

Thank you once again,
Shabbat shalom

❈ ❈ ❈

To: nachum@wfmu.org
Subject: (no subject)

Dear Nachum,
This morning's choice of MBD's "I'd Rather Pray and Sing" had a positive and profound impact on a non-observant friend of mine. Keep it up.

Regards to Staci & Binyamin.
Guten Chodesh

❈ ❈ ❈

To: "'nachum@wfmu.org'" <nachum@wfmu.org>
Subject: Thank You

Nachum,

Meir told me that he emailed you, asking that you mention my father's name on the air. I wanted to share with you something that I have been thinking about for a long time but never had an opportunity to tell you.

I know that my father pulled through last year as a result of very good medical care and, more importantly, the abundance of prayers that were said on his behalf. So many of those tefillot were solely because of you and the chesed you showed, and continue to show, by announcing the names of cholim on the air.

I also know that the chesed you do goes beyond that. You give the families of the cholim, and I know this first hand, something to hold on to. We all pray for our choleh. But you allow us to live with the knowledge that there are countless other people out there who are praying too. And that makes us feel that much less helpless.

I want to thank you from the bottom of my heart for what you have done for us. I pray that b'zchut, in the merit of the kindness you show, Hashem grants you and your family good health and long life. And may you never need such tefillot.

For as long as I can remember, radio has been central to my life. As a kid, I could spend hours mesmerized by a baseball game, sometimes drifting off to sleep with the radio hidden under my pillow. As a teenager, music and talk programs were my favorite ways to end a busy day.

And, for me, the information coming out of that little box was just a fraction of radio's magic. Even more fascinating were the voices that brought that information to my ears. To this day, I am amazed how friendliness and warmth or, on the other hand, hostility and dissent can be conveyed so easily by people whose facial expressions and body language we never see. The ability to convey surprise, excitement, or sadness via words and intonation alone is, in my opinion, truly remarkable.

Conveying emotion is one thing. But even more incredible is radio's ability to *elicit* emotion. How many times have I been awakened by a news bulletin to find myself — within seconds — saddened simply because of the newscaster's tone of voice? How often does a sportscaster's vocal animation make me feel as if I were in the stadium along with 40,000 other fans? How is it that a certain song, playing in the background while I'm attending to other things, influences the pace and mood with which I perform the task at hand?

A longstanding debate in the United States (and elsewhere) stems from the question: Does negative programming affect people's behavior? Producers would like to believe that violence in movies or promiscuity on primetime television has no effect on their viewers. On the other hand, many advocates claim that children inundated with violent programming are more likely to perform violent acts. Some go so far as to blame the media for directly causing criminal behavior.

I'm not sure I would fully agree with any of these statements. But, at the same time, it's hard to fully disagree either. From my vantage point, I cannot deny the powerful effect that the media has on people every day. An email that I received proved to me beyond a shadow of a doubt that what I have believed all along is true, that wholesome, upbeat programming can affect listeners in a positive way.

"Thank you for making my Shabbos so warm. It all started on Friday around 7:30 AM when I was driving to work and was listening to your show. Once I heard the song, "Ko Echsof," from the new album Shabbos Tisch, it went straight into the depths of my neshama. This was a really good start for my Shabbos. Nachum, I'm telling you that it was a different atmosphere at the Shabbos table! What a warm song, filled with dveykus and kedusha. I'm sure you've been mezakeh es harabim (given strength to many). There are a lot of people feeling this way."

Nachum and Meir Weingarten broadcasting from Manhattan Day School on Jerusalem Day

With Malcolm Hoenlein at Manhattan Day School Dinner (Early 2000's). Malcolm has been an integral part of JM in the AM. The Weekly Update on Fridays has been Must Listen Radio for 25 years

I see *JM in the AM* as the Jewish radio show listeners start their day with, or even wake up to. That's why I feel a responsibility to set the proper mood for my audience. When I was a head counselor at Camp Mesorah, a staff member used to joke, "Whatever mood Nachum wakes up in each morning, that's the mood the camp will be in for the day." Just like in summer camp, where I helped set the tone for the day, I want to wake up the portion of the Jewish world I am privileged to greet each morning in a way that will generate a good mood.

Although today's media features constant disagreements between the host and the callers, or between two co-hosts, we go out of our way to avoid that format. In a world where the rude and the outrageous have become synonymous with ratings, where conventional wisdom assumes that to make money there must be constant conflict, we've managed to remain successful with our own approach. We try hard to keep the programming light and upbeat, concentrating more on what we have in common with our listeners than on our disagreements.

I take seriously my responsibility to share Jewish success stories and serve as a positive advertisement for Judaism. I want to be the reminder to all listeners that we should focus on all the good that Judaism and Jews have to offer.

In my interview with Roy Neuberger, I wanted to highlight how special Judaism is that it even has a pull for someone who seemingly has it all and might not look as if he would want to accept all the challenges that come with a religious lifestyle. I asked him to explain why he became religious and what made him give up all that he had achieved for this goal. Roy explained that while it is true that he "had it all" and had successfully attained

With the great Lou Jacobi.

the "American dream," he actually felt like a slave to his lifestyle. And, only in religious Jewish life and sincere service of Hashem did he feel truly free. This was such an important message and I was so happy he could share it so articulately with the audience.

I have had the privilege of interviewing Richie Taylor, the highest-ranking Orthodox Jew in the NYPD, several times on my show and have been so impressed by the way he conducts himself at all times as a representative of the Jewish people. As the first yarmulke-wearing Jew to receive the rank of Deputy Chief, Taylor knows well that many NYPD officers see him as "the Jew." He goes out of his way to forge relationships with people of all religions and backgrounds, maintaining that public safety depends on creating good will among everyone. Sometimes, as a community, we cringe when we see certain people representing us. But when we see Richie Taylor, we are proud to have him work on our behalf and thankful that he is in that position; it is important to get to know people like him.

Even if we are covering a serious topic, we make sure that optimism shines through as much as possible. For example, at the height of the intifadas and Israel's recent wars, most of the media emphasized the constant tragedies, portraying life in Israel as dismal and bleak. In contrast, we decided to broadcast a show directly from Hebron, highlighting its residents' upbeat attitude and underscoring what our listeners could do to help them.

People often ask why I hesitate to announce deaths on the air and usually do so only when a well-known community leader has passed away. I feel strongly that if we begin announcing too much bad news, there will be no end to it and the show's optimism will plummet. To make such announcements with the regularity of our *mazal tov* wishes would detract from our program. And to hear depressing news, listeners can tune into any other media outlet; we want ours to remain happy — within reason.

Because of my appreciation for the power of radio, I purposely do not rehearse with my guests. Most radio hosts prefer to know exactly what to expect from those they will be interacting with on the air. But I think it detracts from the spontaneity of the show. My disbelief, my enthusiasm, or even my disappointment will come across so much more genuinely if it is real and my listeners will know that I am hearing the responses for the first time.

On the one-year anniversary of the tragedy at the Tree of Life Congregation, we broadcasted live from Pittsburgh. Judge Butler had wanted to tell me about the mayor of the city insisting on having the event on the actual anniversary despite the forecast of heavy rain. I would not hear the story before the show as I knew that it would be more impactful live with my immediate reaction instead of pretending to be excited. On the air, Judge Butler told of the *Pittsburgh Gazette's* full-page ad that the mayor had put in that read, "On November 9th 1938, government officials turned their back on the Jews, but on November 9th 2018, we rallied to support our Jewish brethren." It was understood then that he had wanted it on the specific date to highlight the contrast for the Jewish people. It was such a dramatic, heartwarming story with amazing on-air reactions that I was so happy I had not ruined the spontaneity of the interview by hearing the story before the show.

In earlier years, I was careful never to read a book before interviewing the author on the air in order to maintain the spontaneity of the conversation. More recently, I have come to appreciate that reading the book can enhance the interview. But, I still limit conversation before we go on air and will not allow any stories' content to be discussed before we are live.

Our goal is to produce wholesome, respectable programming and I think that our audience appreciates that. As one listener told the *New York Times*, "I can turn on the radio and not worry about what the kids will hear … about rapes, murders, and people being thrown off subway platforms." Somebody recently left me a phone message asking me to announce something. He continued by saying how much he and his father enjoy the show; and he added that we would surely be the ones to announce the arrival of Mashiach, *bimheirah b'yameinu*. His words made my day.

One of our frequent guests is Chabad's Rabbi Mordechai Kanelsky of Hillside, New Jersey. During all his interviews, he never fails to speak highly of his wife, warmly praising her and her wonderful attributes. A few days after one of his appearances, a woman approached Rabbi Kanelsky in a store and said, "The way you speak about your wife is not something that we're used to hearing in our shuls or schools. You should know that because of you, *shalom bayis* (domestic harmony) has increased for Klal Yisrael."

One morning, my wife Staci called in to speak on the air to one of our guests. As she was about to hang up, I said, "I love you." As you can probably guess, the phones in the studio immediately began ringing off the hook; some people were disturbed by such a public display of affection, while others found it refreshing. One woman called to say, "Thank you so much. You don't know what an important lesson this was for the men listening to the show."

Recently, in a letter to the editor in *Mishpacha Magazine*, a man wrote that he is a *baal teshuva* today because listening to "Morning Chizuk" on my show sparked his interest in exploring his roots. After more than forty years in radio, I am more and more aware of this invisible medium's importance. I feel so incredibly lucky to have found a career in that medium, one to which I've been attracted all my life, which is nothing short of providential.

That I have had a role in shaping that medium to foster joy and growth for my listeners is nothing short of miraculous.

SHLOMO CARLEBACH

Subject: reb shlomo & ....
To: nachum@wfmu.org

Hi Nachum!
I really enjoyed your tribute tonight on 620 to Reb Shlomo, zt"l. This yahrzeit is always a bit strange for us, since for the past nine years we also observe our wedding anniversary on this day. It's hard to process that for us, 16 Marcheshvan was the happiest day of our lives, yet it's also a time of such sadness for the Carlebach family and for Klal Yisrael. Remembering and honoring Reb Shlomo have certainly become a part of our anniversary. Through your programs, a part of Shlomo Carlebach — his beautiful, inspirational music — is still very much with us in this world. Thank you for that!!

❋❋❋

To: nachum@wfmu.org
Subject: R. Shlomo Carlebach Z"TL

Nachum,
Mazel tov on the "House of Tomorrow." I was fortunate enough to be in the car when your dear father was talking — a truly satisfying experience!!

I am mailing you a check for $54.00 toward the Shlomo Carlebach yahrzeit memorial.

✻ ✻ ✻

To: nachum@wfmu.org
Subject: Chevron Concert

Reb Nachum,
The Chevron concert was unbelievable. If you looked closely enough, you could see Reb Shlomo on the stage smiling as he saw his music continue to flourish and inspire. What was so special about the concert was the way it characterized Reb Shlomo. The people who walked into Reb Shlomo's shul were from all different backgrounds and walks of life. The performers last night were similar in that respect; each one came from a different background and each one had his own unique way of perpetuating Reb Shlomo's music. The only thing that was missing from the concert was Avraham Rosenblum and a few songs by Diaspora.

The year was 1998, but there was no mistaking that it was him. Though he had left us four years earlier, the one and only Shlomo Carlebach was performing on the stage. *This is it*, I thought, *my chance to ask him for a blessing for more children*; we were not expecting and Staci and I so badly wanted a girl to name for her grandmother, to whom we had been so close. And so, I jumped on stage and asked, "Reb Shlomo, please give me a blessing that Staci and I should have a girl." And he responded in a voice that I can hear so clearly even to this day, "Reb Nachum, what's wrong with three sons?"

And then I awoke. In a sweat, I woke Staci and described what had just happened. Shlomo Carlebach, who had been dead for almost four years, had just spoken to me so lucidly and coherently, as if he had been standing right next to me. It seemed he had revealed to me, albeit in a dream, the

The last time I was with Shlomo Carlebach. Jane and David Seidemann Sheva Brachot (AUG 1994).

genders of our future children. If anyone would have told me this story, I would not have believed it. But it was so real.

The dream had been so authentic and I was so convinced that what he had said had to be true that when a little while later we were expecting triplets and went for a sonogram, I did not need to wait for the technician to reveal the babies' genders. My calculations were clear; if Reb Shlomo had said we would have three sons and we already had one, I was sure that we were expecting one girl and two boys. When the technician told us that the first one was a girl, I said in a tone of voice that revealed there was no reason to continue the procedure, "So now we know that the other two must be boys." The technician thought I was completely crazy until the results showed that I was right. Or, I should say, that Reb Shlomo was right.

From the very beginning, Shlomo Carlebach had held a special place in my heart. Even when I was just starting my radio career and I knew almost nothing about Jewish music, somehow Carlebach stood out. Not only was I aware of his music, I also held it in very high regard. During my first year at *JM in the AM*, I discovered and was inspired by his famous, very long story, "Black Wolf," and decided to play it in its entirety. Since then, I've played it on the air over 200 times, and the response to it is always amazing.

I learned so many things from spending time with Reb Shlomo, not the least of which was his opinion on Jewish music. When I asked him on the air one morning how he felt about the music trends of the early 90's, he first hesitated but then said, in his inimitable style, "Oh, brother, I don't know if I should tell the truth or lie. My bubbie taught me never to lie before ten in the morning, so I'll tell you what I really think." He proceeded to describe the lasting effect of quality music. He criticized those who just copy other genres and merely put Jewish words to them. He emphasized that for music to be good, it must have lasting value. When I pointed out that one of his newer songs sounded much like one of his older ones, he replied, "Everyone else steals my songs, why can't I?"

Another important character trait that I learned from Reb Shlomo was his complete disregard for materialism. Regardless of how much or how little money he had, he never altered his lifestyle or let it affect anything about him. By his example, he taught that spirituality is the only important quality. As a deeply spiritual man, he wanted to use his music to bridge the gap between people.

I had the opportunity to host this legendary Jew many times. In one interview he described how, in 1967, he had begged members of the Israeli government to allow him to be an emissary of peace. He was convinced that if he were permitted to go with his friends into Arab villages and just play music together, peace would follow. Opposing religious coercion, Reb Shlomo advocated offering a Shabbos experience for those who frequented Israeli coffee houses rather than demanding that the coffee houses be forced to close on Shabbos. He felt the best way to inspire people to become more religious was through music and sincere friendship.

I tried to spend as much time as possible with him, grabbing even a few minutes before introducing him at a concert or offering to drive him when he needed a ride. During our many travels, he taught me how to lead the *Selichos* prayers. Now, each year when I daven for the *amud*, I remember what a privilege it was to have learned from the master.

What is truly amazing — and from a professional standpoint, this is simply incredible — is that Reb Shlomo's music appeals to people from across the Jewish spectrum. While I usually must make a programming choice between an artist who appeals to one segment of my audience versus another, Carlebach transcends all boundaries. I know that the less observant, even those not observant at all, want to hear him — and so do those who are very religious.

Many people know of Reb Shlomo's involvement with less-affiliated Jews, be it through performances in the Catskills in the '50s, San Francisco's House of Love and Prayer in the '60s, or even his Manhattan synagogue, known simply as The Carlebach Shul. However, many are unaware that he was a tremendous Torah scholar. Every time I met him, he had a *sefer*, a holy book, in his hand. He always had a Chassidic tale or lesson to share with me — and I always wondered what his scholarly German ancestors might have thought of those ideas. He was truly brilliant. One time when he was in the studio, a listener called and asked him, "Why don't you stop talking about your music and tell everyone what a big *talmid chacham* you are?" Of course, he denied it, but those in the know were fully aware that it was true.

Staci and I felt so lucky to have had Shlomo Carlebach perform at our wedding. I remember that he played two songs: something from the Yom Kippur davening and his classic, *"Kah Ribon."* I simply couldn't figure out why he chose those songs. Years later, I asked him on the air about his two selections. Reb Shlomo explained that one's wedding day is like Yom Kippur and that he thought that *Kah Ribon* was his best waltz, which he found apropos for the setting.

Through all the great times we shared, I never imagined that one day I'd be announcing his death on the air. But on Friday morning, October 21, 1994, to the astonishment of most of my listeners, I opened the show by saying, "I have tragic news to share with everybody: Shlomo Carlebach has died of a heart attack at the age of 69."

Moments later, we began to play Reb Shlomo's music and then opened the phones, allowing people to share their grief and their memories with each other. Famous dignitaries and just plain folks, people whose lives he had touched and those who had never known him — all called to express their sorrow.

Since then, each year on Reb Shlomo's yahrzeit, we devote the entire show to this legend in his own time. On the day after Tisha B'Av, when many do not listen to music, we broadcast his stories in their entirety. And on many occasions throughout the year, we invite his friends, relatives, and colleagues to speak about his life and his extraordinary endeavors. In short, we attempt to ensure that the music and the lessons of Reb Shlomo Carlebach continue to live on, not only in my dreams but in the hearts and minds of all our listeners.

JEWISH UNITY INITIATIVE

In 2015, when the terror attack that took place in a kosher supermarket in Paris resulted in the murder of four innocent Jews, we saw the attack on the third-largest Jewish community in the world as an attack on Jewish communities everywhere. We felt that we had to do more to show support for the Jews of Paris, and we immediately contacted the communal organization, the Consistoire in Paris, saying that we wanted to come and host a show and concert that would express solidarity. They thought it was too early, because people were still mourning and many would be too afraid to leave their homes. A few months later, with their permission, we started working on our gift to the Jews of Paris — a free concert open to all. We flew to Paris to arrange the logistics, brought producer Dovid Fadida from Israel, and selected Yehoram Gaon and Ohad to be the featured singers. We decided to host the concert in the Great Synagogue of Paris; we had a stage built there and brought in a complete sound and lighting team.

To commemorate the one-year anniversary of the attack, on the fourth night of Chanukah, we invited the whole community and specifically welcomed the families of those killed in the attacks. Yeshiva University President Rich-

Staci and an IDF soldier protecting the JM in the AM tour bus, Israel 1990.

ard Joel joined us there, and the Chief Rabbi of Paris spoke. We asked the chairman of the event, Robert Ben Rimon, to represent our team and sponsors and deliver the keynote message because he speaks French, and we wanted the community to feel fully welcomed and engaged. The concert was broadcast around the world and we were interviewed on Paris news stations about the event. It was a very moving concert and its impact was realized immediately. It was described by a supporter as "3,000 Parisians enjoying the night and feeling love from people on the other side of the world." The Rabbi of the Great Synagogue said that people would remember the night for a very long time; I run into people all the time who recognize us from there and cannot stop thanking us for all that we accomplished.

Two NSN supporters, Simon Jacob and Dr. Joe Rozehzadeh, flew to Paris to be a part of the event; they were so impressed that they became founders and key players in what would come to be known as our Jewish Unity Initiative, an initiative expressing care and solidarity to communities around the world. With the success of the Paris event, we set out to find other ways that we could make an impact.

In November 2016, Miriam and I both noticed a *New York Times* article about the Jewish community of Venice celebrating the five-hundredth anniversary of the Venetian Ghetto. We wanted to show our support and again organized a free concert, bringing in a production team and singers from Israel and inviting the whole community to join. It is a very small community, but everyone came. Even those factions of the community who do not always see eye to eye set aside their differences for the night and joined together for an enjoyable evening of unity, proving how big an impact a Jewish music event can have.

At the 2012 launch of The Nachum Segal Network with YU President Richard Joel.

Listeners began to ask where we were going next. We saw the importance of conveying to communities in need that we care about them; by highlighting them in these big events, we bring to our listeners' attention the importance of offering financial help to Jews in need, regardless of the location.

When Hurricane Harvey flooded Houston, the Jewish community was hit very hard. We flew out to Houston and broadcasted a show from there, speaking to community

*JNF's Russel Robinson presenting a "tree" certificate.
I told him we are not a network if we don't have trees planted in our honor.*

members about what they were experiencing and how others could help. Listeners commented that not only was this helpful to those in Houston, but it was helpful to the audience as well, as it allowed them to feel the pain of fellow Jews suffering many miles away.

In 2016, when Israel was struck by a string of random stabbings, we wanted to demonstrate the enduring importance of visiting Israel and to express solidarity with them during their struggles. But we did not want to just visit; we wanted to show the unity of the Jewish people. So, we chose four different locations, each representing a different segment of the Israeli community, and broadcasted a show from each. We were in the Old City in Jerusalem, in Dizengoff Square in Tel Aviv, at the Pina Chama in the Gush, and in Sderot, the community closest to the border with Gaza. The feedback we received was heartwarming and inspiring.

With Miriam and Mark, the core of our parade broadcast team.

Following the October 2018 Pittsburgh shooting inside the Tree of Life Synagogue, listeners assumed that we were going to broadcast from there; by now we knew how important it was to go and show solidarity. We hosted a show that focused on what the Pittsburgh community had experienced and provided information about how others around the world could show their unity. We were grateful for the opportunity to show that we cared. But perhaps equally impactful was our ability to bring the suffering of the community to people around the world. It was no longer something they were reading about from far away. As we interviewed members of the community and described what we were seeing, it made it real for the audience, resulting in more caring and generous responses.

In December 2020, following the Abraham Accords, the historic agreement normalizing ties between Israel and the United Arab Emirates, Ariella

Steinreich, a longtime fan and friend of the show who had always been involved with the UAE, suggested that we travel there to tell the story for our listeners. We were awed when we landed in what looked like a futuristic city and immediately began broadcasting from there. We interviewed local Arab leaders and business people and discussed their incredible successes, which they attributed to their open-minded attitude toward all people and their zero tolerance for crime and terrorism.

We met with local Jewish leaders, as well, and they told us that they feel respected by the Arab community and even more so when they stay true to their values, such as wearing a yarmulke in public. We were joined for part of the trip by Jason Greenblatt, President Trump's Special Representative for International Negotiations, who had helped broker the Abraham Accords.

The trip was truly eye-opening and we felt it was so important to bring the experience to our listeners and share the lessons learned. As an average Jewish American who grew up in the day-school system, I perceived Arabs as people who wanted to destroy Israel and hated Jews. I know that I, and I think this is shared among most people I know, never had encountered Arabs who craved peace and prosperity. We discovered a whole segment of the Arab community who feel there is much to be gained from peaceful relations with Israel, and they bemoan the fact that much of their neighborhood in the Middle East does not allow it.

It is hard to believe until you experience it that there are people in the Arab world who respect Israel. We felt so privileged to introduce to our audience these legitimate peace partners who hope that one day it will be more popular in their region to be pro-Israel than against.

Lipa at the Kosher Halftime Show 2016.

These journeys, and others, including to places around the United States and Israel, have produced broadcasts that reflect the mission of Jewish unity. They allow listeners to hear firsthand what others are going through, and they allow us to demonstrate solidarity and care to communities that generally do not receive our close attention. Jewish Unity and the Jewish Unity Initiative are key components of the Nachum Segal Network, and we feel privileged to have been a part of these projects.

TOP TEN

To: <Nachum@wfmu.org>

I listen to your JM in the AM every morning and The Nachum Segal Show every evening on my commute between my home in Kew Gardens Hills, Queens, and my office in Stamford, CT.

Frankly, I lose the transmission in parts of CT (which frustrates me immensely!).

Keep up the good work! Can't wait till you get a stronger signal!!

To: <nachum@wfmu.org>
Subject: JM in the AM

Hi, Nachum. I enjoy your show so much, especially since I drive eight children from Huntington (Suffolk County, Long Island) to Queens to their various yeshivas in the morning. There is only one problem: the reception is so weak! I can only access the show in the heart of Queens, and every other minute, you fade out/in. Can the signal somehow be strengthened?

Yours is the only radio show I feel is kosher — and enjoyable — to keep on in the car with children! Please help!

❊❊❊

To: nachum@wfmu.org
Subject: Talking

Dear Nachum,
I am an avid listener of both your shows, in the morning and evening, and I enjoy them tremendously. The music is really uplifting.

I just would like to make an observation: I love the music very much, but the TALKING is too much and too long. Most of the time I tune out and check back if the music is back on.

❊❊❊

To: nachum@wfmu.org
Subject: My son-in-law

I am sure you have heard of him and probably know him personally, too. He is a very talented young man and works very hard at writing beautiful songs. Perhaps you could have him on your show too? He is in the middle of putting together new songs for his second CD. Thanks for any attention/help you can give him. Have a great day!

❋ ❋ ❋

To: nachum@wfmu.org

Today at work, I offered to resign (though I was ignored). The import/impact of your plans had hit me (namely, the fact you plan on making aliyah, IY"H, next year).

I guess it's true of all public figures, people are curious to know more about them. Questions abound: What keeps them busy behind the scenes? How much of what they do or say is actually "for real"? What do they do when they are not in the public eye (or, in my case, ear)? It's funny to think of myself in that kind of position, but it seems that over the years I have become the subject of questions like these.

When I am on the road or even in my own neighborhood, people often approach me with a question about my life; their tone of voice underscores that their question has been bothering them for quite some time. Following my reply, their voices often convey gratitude that a long-standing mystery has been resolved. On the other hand, many listeners are uncomfortable approaching me or simply don't have an opportunity to see me. Sometimes, those individuals make a beeline to members of either my staff or my family, peppering them with queries — some about what I do on the air and some about my life off the air.

Over the years, those closest to me have noticed that many of these questions recur. Robert Katz, one of my substitute hosts and lifelong friend, got together with other members of my broadcasting team and compiled what has come to be known as "The Top Ten Questions Asked about Nachum Segal." Here they are:

10. Is it true that he is making *aliyah*?

Ever since I married Staci, rumors have been circulating about where we will be relocating. When we moved to the Lower East Side, generally viewed as a transient community, people began speculating about our next destination. When we spend Shabbos in a community other than our own, I'm often asked the following week if we are checking it out for ourselves. I once innocently asked someone about housing prices in Brooklyn; instantly, rumors began to fly that we were planning to move there.

As for making *aliyah*, I'm certainly excited about this specific rumor. At least it has had some positive results; I've heard people say that if a regular guy like Nachum is moving to Israel, they can probably do it, too. If I am in any way responsible for the popularity of *aliyah* — if only as a topic of conversation — I couldn't be happier. If just one person thinks that *aliyah* isn't such a crazy concept simply because he heard that I am taking that step, I couldn't be happier. I love being in Israel as often as I can but, for now, we have no concrete plans to move there permanently.

9. Is the fundraising marathon rigged?

The annual fundraising marathon, which we did with WFMU until we parted in 2016, was not rigged. If it were, then I wouldn't have lost countless hours of sleep worrying about its outcome. Many people noticed that we always seemed to reach our goal on the final day. That is simply because our most generous supporters chose to wait until Marathon Friday to announce their pledges. Perhaps they liked the dramatic effect, perhaps they did not want me to be able to eat all week; either way, it was certainly their prerogative. After all those years at the job, my good friends and colleagues, Mattes Weingast and Mark Zomick, had gotten the fundraising system down to a science. Maybe that is why what was really an honest endeavor might have appeared otherwise.

Many listeners wonder how we consistently reached (or almost reached) our financial goal each year. My only answer is that I kept on praying! Anyone who saw me or any member of my staff during those weeks in February could tell from our baggy eyes and worried dispositions that we were very uncertain about the outcome.

8. Is he alone in the studio?

In the morning I am usually alone in the studio (who else would be crazy enough to wake up that early?) I work the console, manage the technical equipment, sit alone at the microphone, and am responsible for station identification, not to mention anything else that goes into making a radio show run smoothly.

This is out of the ordinary for a radio show. Most hosts have at least some sort of technical staff and other team members responsible for various tasks. Because I started my radio career in a station with such a low budget, that's what I got used to from the beginning; I've been able to manage like this ever since. Except when it is obvious that I am addressing a guest in the studio, all the interviews are conducted over the phone and the guest segments, such as Rabbi Yudin's "Torah Thought of the Week," are pre-recorded.

7. Why can't he play more music?

As often as I hear this question, I hear just as many — if not more — requests by individuals, groups, and organizations who want to appear on the show. Unfortunately, I cannot say yes to all of them; if I did, there would be no time for music at all. At the same time, the show is designed to serve its audience by providing *Divrei Torah*, mazal tov announcements, and news reports, not to mention airtime to organizations that aid different segments of our community.

It is hard to strike the right balance, especially with so little time, so much to cover, and so many requests for airtime. We are fully aware that it is impossible to please all our listeners all the time. We just keep trying to do our best.

6. Is his wife a saint?

Yes.

5. Why does he talk when he is playing "*Hatikvah*"?

I have often been asked how I could speak during the playing of the Israeli National Anthem. I definitely understand why people would see this as offensive, and anyone who knows me knows that I appreciate the seriousness of "*Hatikvah*." I answer that I do not play it as a song for entertainment but simply as a radio theme to end each show.

4. Why can't I hear the show where I live? And why do I hear it better in the car than in the house?

Though this question has become outdated in the internet era, for the first 25 years of the show, this was perhaps the question that I was asked most frequently. Most people did not realize the prohibitive costs involved in expanding a radio station's listening radius. I considered it a miracle that G-d guided me, at twenty years of age, to a station that reaches so many people with such a low budget. It was truly providential that a small college radio station reaches far beyond its campus's borders all the way to the Jewish communities of New York and New Jersey. If Upsala College had been located elsewhere, it would have been virtually useless to us. In the New York metropolitan area, where it costs millions of dollars to produce most radio shows, it was nothing short of miraculous that we were able to broadcast for three hours a day with a relatively modest budget.

There is always better reception in open areas, so it stood to reason that it was easier to hear our show while in a car. That it was possible to hear the show at all in Nassau County and other remote areas — even if only in the car — was truly unbelievable.

3. How can I get on the show?

It is very difficult to formulate an answer to this question because so many factors go into making these decisions — and in the end it comes down to our judgment. We try to balance Israeli causes with American ones, to give lesser-known organizations a chance to be heard, and to help the larger ones as well. We offer airtime to organizations our listeners want to hear about, and we give slots to those causes they would never hear of if it weren't for our broadcast.

Sometimes the decision is based on credentials, sometimes on references, sometimes on the length of time we've been in contact, and sometimes simply on a hunch that something will be new and interesting to our listeners. For every person or organization featured on the show, fifty are excluded — not because they are unworthy but because if we invited everyone on the air, no time would remain for music.

2. From this he makes a living?

I've been so fortunate to have always had a supportive family. When I first launched my radio career, my parents were unconditionally encouraging, never questioning how I would make enough money or what would happen if I did not succeed in such a competitive field. Even my father, who I thought would never be excited about radio, was intrigued by the idea from the moment he heard my first show.

When Staci and I married, I found myself living in an equally supportive environment. While many wives might demand that their husbands get a "real job," Staci has always been exceedingly patient with and tolerant of the unique schedule that accompanies the career I've chosen. While we both knew it wouldn't be easy, she and I were both willing to live on a smaller salary so that I could continue doing what I love.

As any Torah-observant parent knows, after a certain number of kids, that type of thinking goes from difficult to virtually impossible. The many financial constraints that accompany raising a large Jewish family convinced me that I would soon have to give up my dream job and get into a normal career, making a living like every other good Jewish husband and father.

I benefited greatly from the forethought and expertise of Ken Freedman, WFMU's general manager. In addition, my younger brother Yigal helped me establish both my website and my business so that I could continue in radio without too much sacrifice. I know I could be earning more by pursuing a different career. I know some people are baffled by my choices. Still, I am willing — and, luckily, Staci is willing as well — to live on a little less so that I can continue doing what I love.

1. When does he daven?

The answer that I always give to this most frequent question is, "Before, during or after the show, depending on the day."

My words are a bit vague because, in fact, my davening schedule does fluctuate, depending on the schedules of the present and previous days. But they are also vague because this question usually is accompanied by a hint of judgment: *Why are you giving yourself permission to forego praying with a minyan? Why are you giving yourself permission to maintain such an erratic prayer schedule?*

My words are *not* vague, because praying with a minyan is not something I take lightly, G-d forbid. Anyone who knows me knows that davening, particularly with a minyan, is something that I take very seriously; in fact, when away from the studio, I am particularly diligent about davening in shul. But I do not take my broadcasting responsibilities lightly either. *Baruch Hashem*, those responsibilities have enriched the lives of so many Jews, both affiliated and unaffiliated, and that is something I cherish.

I once asked Rabbi Goldwasser about this matter. He replied, "If you were to consider giving up what you're doing in order to attend a minyan each morning, you would have a serious *shailah* (rabbinic question) on your hands."

I thank him for that.

HOW WOULD YOU LIKE YOUR SHOW?

To: Nachum@wfmu.org
Subject: the millennium

Dear Nachum,
I enjoy listening to you in the morning. I've noticed, however, that you promote the HASC concert as the first concert of the new millennium and emphasize the appropriateness of this.

I'd like to remind you that the "millennium" is significant only to Christians as it represents the 2,000th anniversary of the birth of Jesus. When you refer to the "millennium," it is definitely not a "Jewish moment." Please develop an appropriately Jewish means of promoting the HASC concert.

Thank you for an otherwise excellent program.

To: Nachum@wfmu.org
Subject: Feedback on Programming

Nachum,
I listen to JM in the AM (what does "JM" stand for, anyway?) when commuting to work in Poughkeepsie, NY, picking up the station from the Catskills. One thing that I have noticed is that there can be DAYS going by without any female singers. Is this realistic? I KNOW that there are female singers out there (Debbie Friedman, for example)! It would be nice if you can give them some air time as well.

Thank you.

❋❋❋

To: nachum@wfmu.org
Subject: KAIN AYIN HARA

Dear Nachum,
Your show is great but I have a bone to pick with you. When you say KAIN AYIN HORA, to Israelis it sounds like YES-AYIN HARA, MEANING THAT the ayin hara should befall someone. Try saying BLEE AYIN HORA. It sounds better.

Regards.

❋❋❋

To: nachum@wfmu.org

Good morning. Every morning and evening I listen to your great radio show and really enjoy it!

A few times while I was listening to JM in the AM and I heard u playing music of a woman singing. I don't know if you're aware of the issur of a man hearing a woman singing (I'm sure you do). I'm a girl and this bothers me a lot — imagine a man, how much more so! Just think about it, if a man happens to have seen a picture of that lady, do you know what an issur it is for him?!? I don't think you want to be held responsible — after one hundred and twenty — for all the men that you were machshel —for just even three minutes. I'm sorry if I sound like this aidel knaidel, but I just wanted to bring this to your attention.

Thanks for taking the time to read this annoying letter!

Subject: Programming
To: nachum@wfmu.org

Dear Nochum,
It was a pleasure getting your station up in the mountains. The music in the morning is a very good boost on any morning. It helps for a more relaxed day.

The following is not only my opinion, but the opinion of others I work with, too. At times, you interview people. Sometimes the interview is important. It is an avenue of information, such as the Iranian 10 or in-depth issues concerning Israel.

However, at times you have repeated guests, with underlying self-interests (this is not only my opinion). The issues discussed are repetitious at times, and that is when we choose to turn to another station or turn on a tape.

Being we live in stressful times and mornings can baruch Hashem be very stressful, could you please stick to music?

Perhaps send out a questionnaire with your yearly campaign.

A K'siva V'Chasima Tova.

In my years as a radio host, I've noticed that people become so personally attached to the show that they come to think it is about them. Following last year's Celebrate Israel Parade, I received a call from a listener asking why I hadn't given her specific school more attention than others, attention she was sure her school deserved. One of the most fascinating phenomena has been the plethora of people expressing varied, and sometimes opposing,

Nachum Segal (Springdale Avenue, East Orange, NJ, Studio)

opinions about how the show should be run. It's never been bothersome to me; in fact, I've always felt flattered that people cared enough to write. But I've often found it amusing; in fact, I've often wondered how each of these callers, letter writers, and email correspondents — knowing full well how diverse our listening audience is — envisioned my tailoring the show to his or her precise specifications.

With all the requests for programming changes, ranging from general policies to very specific details, I've joked about creating a listener questionnaire. It might look something like this:

1. **During *Sefirah* (period of communal mourning), I should play:**
   A. No music at all from Pesach to Shavuos — if anybody isn't permitted to hear music, then nobody should.

Best view ever, from the Aish HaTorah balcony (thank you, Rabbi Steven Burg)! February 2016 broadcast.

    B. Regular music from Pesach to Shavuos — people can follow their personal custom and can be trusted not to listen to the radio when they are not supposed to.

    C. Only a cappella music — even though I realize that fast a cappella songs are more festive than slow songs with instrumental accompaniment, that's what my friends are doing, so it works for me.

2. **When referring to an event that is taking place after Shabbat, I should say that it will be on:**

    A. *Motza'ei Shabbos* — the show should have a familiar, Jewish sound to it.

    B. Saturday night — listeners who are not familiar with Hebrew need to hear more English on the show.

    C. Both *Motza'ei Shabbos* and Saturday night — even though it would

Hosting with Miriam & ZK from The Inbal Hotel. The Inbal continues to be our Jerusalem headquarters. Thank you to Rony Timset and his great staff.

result in very wordy, tedious sentences, each word of the show should be said in both languages to satisfy all.

3. When I receive a request to highlight a specific communal organization on the air, I should:
   A. Only do it if the cause interests most listeners — otherwise, they will tune out.
   B. Only do it if it will introduce a new cause to most listeners — otherwise, they will tune out.
   C. Only do it if the cause interests most of the audience, but please make an exception for *my* cause — it is such an important one.

4. **When scheduling the different segments of the show, I should:**
   A. Always play the news at the same time, the *d'var Torah* at the same

With Rabbi Shlomo Katz at Jewish Unity Initiative broadcast in Gush Etzion.

time, and the mazal tovs at the same time — then I'll know when to turn on the radio.

B. Switch the scheduling each day — that way, I can hear a variety of programming in the daily time slot available to me to hear the show.

C. Switch the programming each day — but make sure to announce the mazal tovs at 8:30 on Tuesdays, because that's when I do carpool.

5. **If we have too much news to cover and must choose between a local story or an Israeli story, we should:**

A. Always choose the Israeli story — I can tune in to any other radio station for local news.

B. Always choose the local story — I don't listen to any other radio

One of our favorite live show locations—The good ole Homowack Hotel. Ann and Pinny Davidman (and the Ash family) were great hosts.

station, so I'd like to hear what is most pertinent to me.

C. Choose neither — I prefer more music and less talk.

6. **Regarding news about Yeshiva League sports, I should:**
   A. Never speak about it — I send my children to schools that do not play organized sports, and I don't want you to expose them to the concept.
   B. Give it as much coverage as possible — my son's hockey games are the most important events in our lives, and I want to relive them as often as possible.
   C. I don't even know what Yeshiva League sports is, but anything that means more news and less music — I'm all for it.

7. **Regarding funeral announcements, we should:**

The Team (2013)

    A. Never broadcast them — they would ruin the show's upbeat atmosphere.
    B. Always broadcast them — that will give the greatest number of people the opportunity to attend the funeral.
    C. Never broadcast them — they would get out of hand and ruin the show's upbeat atmosphere — but make an exception for my friend or relative's funeral announcement.

8. **When we get a request to play a song performed by a woman, we should:**
    A. Definitely play it, completely ignoring the sensitivities of all those who do not want to hear it.
    B. Definitely not play it, completely ignoring the talents of 50% of

With JUI Co-Chair, Simon Jacob.

    the world's population.
- **C.** Try to appease everybody by playing it, but very infrequently, thereby upsetting all listeners.

9. **While on the air, I should use a tone of voice that is:**
   - **A.** Very jovial — this is a radio show and it should be entertaining.
   - **B.** Very serious — too much joking around creates a mockery of Jewish life.
   - **C.** Somewhere in between — maybe a few less jokes than yesterday and a few more than today. Last Thursday's show was perfect except for the 7:30 - 8:00 slot, which could have used a little more enthusiasm.

With Staci at historic Synagogue of Venice - JUI November 2016.

10. When choosing which music to play on a regular basis, we should:
   A. Play only Shlomo Carlebach — everything else sounds so not Jewish.
   B. Play only MBD and Avraham Fried — everything else sounds so not Jewish.
   C. Play only the brand-new artists with a real feel for what young people want to hear — everything else sounds so not Jewish.
   D. Play only klezmer — everything else sounds so not Jewish.
   E. Play only cantorial selections — everything else sounds so not Jewish.
   F. Play only Israeli songs — everything else sounds so not Jewish.

In all seriousness, I have received most of these requests, in one form or another, countless times. I've asked other radio hosts if they receive similar

JUI co-chairs, Lori & Dr Joe Rozezadeh, in Venice.

critiques and suggestions. Their replies have confirmed that our show receives an inordinate amount of commentary. At one point, I began to take it personally, worrying that perhaps I was not producing a quality broadcast; after all, so many listeners were unhappy with so much of it.

When I shared my concern with Rabbi Dovid Goldwasser, a long-time friend and a daily presenter on the show, he put a whole new spin on these well-meaning criticisms. Listeners, he explained, do not consider our show to be like any other radio broadcast; that is, as a show produced solely by the host. Instead, they feel such a personal connection to it that they perceive it as *their* show. And if it is their show, they want it to reflect their individual tastes; if it doesn't, they feel compelled to make the necessary adjustments.

Trip to flood-ravaged Houston, with Mordechai Shapiro.

I sincerely appreciate my listening audience's devotion. Still, from the outset of my radio career, I've been determined to maintain the show's professionalism. So when I receive requests to announce lost-and-found items, broadcast detailed birthday wishes, or play a new song composed by someone's relative, I must keep in mind the long-term goals of the show.

I am happy to implement many of my listeners' suggestions. And at the same time, I feel bad each time I'm forced to say no to someone who wants to speak on the show or change its policies or programming. One thing keeps me on an even keel: remembering the vast variety that comprises my listening audience. That is what enables me to choose programming based on its ability to appeal to an extremely diverse population.

How do I make those choices? So far, a combination of good judgment, natural intuition, and experience has served me well. Unquestionably, my listeners' suggestions and critiques have been invaluable, helping me to assess what is needed and wanted by our community. I just wish people would understand that not everybody pronounces words, observes *Sefiras Ha'Omer*, or, for that matter, listens to the radio, exactly the way they do.

JM IN THE AM TRADITIONS

Over the years, *JM in the AM* has become such an established entity that we have developed a daily and an annual set of guidelines that have become an important part of what the listening community experiences on a regular basis, giving the show an air of predictability and a sense of continuity and tradition. Regular repetition in radio is a vital part of the success of the medium, and it is certainly an integral way of promoting the values that I convey on the air. The following list of our daily and annual traditions [inspired by my niece, Tikva Adler] reflects the values I feel are important and which my listening community has come to expect. It gives a sense of how vital consistency is in a live radio presentation.

JM in the AM Traditions:

Modeh Ani (M-F 6 a.m.)
When I first started the show in 1983, I felt that it was important to start every morning radio show the same way that Jews start their day, by thanking G-d for giving them the gift of waking up. The version that I chose had recently been released by Regesh and became very popular.

192 | JM IN THE AM TRADITIONS

The camera bag of Mr Israel Shaya Dear. Our amazing friend, Mr Dear, took hundreds of photos with that bag being held by celebrities and influential people.

Over the years, some listeners have asked to replace it with a newer version, but I think that most people appreciate the predictability of the show's opening.

Galei Zahal News Broadcast (M-F 7 a.m.)
This is a three-minute live news broadcast, fully in Hebrew, from the IDF radio station. While the Hebrew might be frustrating for some, I feel it is important to offer this shared exposure, so that my audience can hear what people are listening to in Israel. In Israel, people are listening to this broadcast in their cars and their kitchens. Meanwhile, Jews around the world can feel connected by listening in.

Morning Chizuk with Rabbi Dovid Goldwasser (M-TH 7:30 a.m.)
Rabbi Goldwasser was already giving his daily *d'var Torah* when I came to WFMU in 1983. I like to say that I inherited him. People always enjoyed

and found meaning in his presentations, and I felt lucky to have him on the team. Over the years, my family and I have become very close to him and he has been incredibly helpful in many ways. His "Morning Chizuk" has continued to be enjoyable and meaningful to our wide range of listeners; I dedicated the segment in memory of my parents when they passed away.

Acheinu B'Yisrael Anachnu Imachem/Our Brothers and Sisters in Israel, We are with You (M-F 8:58 a.m.)

In 1988, at the beginning of the first Intifada in Israel, I started including this message toward the end of every show. I felt that it was important for my listeners all over the world to feel connected and to feel a responsibility toward our brothers and sisters living in Israel who were experiencing the daily attacks and bombings. I never felt it was appropriate to remove this message, because we should always be attuned to what is happening in Israel, even in peaceful times.

"Hatikvah" (M-F 8:59 a.m.)

I have always felt the importance of the Israeli National Anthem being heard by as many people as possible and that it becomes familiar to all. Though my listening audience is varied in their relationship with the State of Israel, everyone understands why I play it. They know who I am and they respect my staying true to my values.

Remember the Past, Live the Present, Trust the Future (M-F 9:00 a.m.)

In 1985, I wanted to find a meaningful and captivating phrase to end the show. When I went to Israel, I brought along a notebook in which I wrote ideas and quotes that I saw and heard around the country. When I got home, I read the list to my father and as I was reading this one, he jumped up, excited that this was the right fit. I had seen it written on the wall of the Museum of the Diaspora in Tel Aviv and it sums up an important Jewish approach: remembering where we came from, maximizing the time we have, and acknowledging our trust in the Providence of the One Above.

"*Maasecha Hashem*" (Monday 6:05 a.m.)

What better way to begin every new work week than with the acknowledgment that Hashem's world is beautiful? This song by Meir Sherman reminds us of the omnipresence of our Creator and the beauty of His creations. I felt the song is the perfect way to begin a workweek that might include challenges and frustrations. It reminds us of how great a world He has given us and is a great way to keep these things in perspective.

Yeshiva League Sports Update with Elliot Weiselberg (Tuesday 7:20 a.m.)

There was a time when this update was one of the few addresses for news in the Yeshiva League. Now there are many other ways to hear the updates and find out information. But kids, parents, and schools still like being mentioned on the air, and they feel their efforts are more official when reported in this segment.

Harry Rothenberg on the *Parasha* (Friday 7:10 a.m.)

Harry Rothenberg, a prominent attorney who is very involved in Jewish outreach, is a recent addition to the show who brings to the audience a unique take on the *parsha* (Torah portion of the week). It is always concise and with a contemporary message that listeners appreciate. Harry takes everyday situations that may not seem scholarly or biblical and relates them to the week's Torah portion in new and interesting ways.

Weekly Update with Malcolm Hoenlein (Friday 7:40 a.m.)

Malcolm Hoenlein, the vice chairman of the Conference of Presidents of Major American Jewish Organizations, had appeared on the show periodically for many years. After 9/11, we turned it into a weekly spot. The key to the overwhelming success of this segment and its appeal to so many is a combination of Hoenlein's vast knowledge and my insistence on always asking questions that the average listener would ask. The regularity and length of this segment highlight that there is always something going on in the world that affects Israel and the Jewish world. Actually, this station was the first place, in the 1990s, in which Malcolm expressed his concerns about the rise of Islamic fundamentalism and the danger it posed to the free world.

Rabbi Benjamin Yudin's Torah Portion (Friday and Erev Yom Tov 8:15 a.m.)

A well-known and well-liked rabbi, Rabbi Yudin, had also been at WFMU before I got there. I felt a *d'var Torah* on the *parsha* was a must; when I was informed how popular the young rabbi already was on the radio, I was happy to have Rabbi Yudin deliver it each week. He has already celebrated his fortieth anniversary on the air, and over those decades his segment has become a vital part of so many listeners' Erev Shabbos and Yom Tov experiences.

Candle Lighting Times (Friday and Erev Yom Tov)

There are still listeners whose only source of information regarding candle-lighting times comes from *JM in the AM*. Since we have become a global entity, I try to emphasize that the times we are announcing are for the New York area. Hopefully, this encourages listeners around the world to find out what time Shabbos starts wherever they are. In the summer, I also use the opportunity to remind listeners that some communities begin Shabbos earlier, and in the winter, I remind people that Friday is very short and that they should prepare accordingly.

"Time to Say Good Shabbos" (Friday 8:55 a.m.)

We had other songs to conclude the week before this one. But, as soon as Journeys released this song, I knew it was the perfect song to close out the week. "Throw away your hammer" and its related phrases create a spiritual transition from the work week to the upcoming beautiful Shabbos. When listeners hear this song played on *JM in the AM*, they know that the week's finish line is in sight.

Shofar Blowing (Elul)

Not everyone goes to synagogue, and I wanted those who do not to also feel the spiritual awakening that the Elul shofar-blowing provides. We play a simple recording of the sounds that are being blown in synagogues around the world. We do not expect our recording to replace the authentic experience, but at least it offers the opportunity to feel the season's heightened sense of repentance.

Chessed Campaigns (Tishrei and Nisan)

I take these opportunities, before the two holiday seasons, to promote ways to help those in need. These are the times when people are most focused on giving and when the poor are in the greatest need of charity. The Chessed Campaigns include ways to fund needy families' basic holiday necessities and ways to make the holidays more enjoyable and fun for the children of our community.

Tu B'Shvat Special

On the day that we celebrate the earliest blooming trees in the Land of Israel, it would be easy to forget the day entirely as we are mired in the dead of winter in most of the world. We try to highlight the way that it is celebrated in Israel through music and conversation so that we bridge the gap and feel better connected to the Holy Land.

Comedy Segments (Adar)

Old-time comedy routines from the mid-20th century are an annual *JM in the AM* favorite, bringing the laugh-out-loud spirit of Adar to our listeners. Whether they are laughing or groaning, listeners cannot get enough of these segments, and we often receive communications asking for more.

Cancer Screening Reminders (4 Adar)

On my brother's yahrzeit, the day he succumbed to cancer, I take the opportunity to remind our listeners of the importance of screenings. Because of my brother's experience, I emphasize that an endoscopy and colonoscopy must be done on a regular basis. Over the years, I have received feedback from many grateful people telling me that these reminders have actually led to lives saved.

Pesach Products Program (Nisan)

To help listeners properly prepare for Pesach, a panel of rabbis and pharmacists takes questions from the audience. Listeners avail themselves of this unique opportunity to ask about the kosher-for-Pesach status of their medications, pet food, cosmetics, and, of course, regular food items. In addition to being informative, this segment, always a favorite of WFMU general manager Ken Freedman, has had many entertaining moments over the years, reflective of just how jovial Passover preparation can be.

Siyum, Completion of a Unit of Torah Study (Erev Pesach)

As the first-born males in our community are not permitted to eat on Erev Pesach unless they participate in a *siyum*, there are thousands of *siyumim* conducted in synagogues around the world on that morning. We conduct a *siyum* on the air, not because it will allow people to eat, but because we feel that if the entire Jewish world is performing a ritual on the same day, we should do the same on the air.

Omer-Counting Reminder

I try to utilize every opportunity to help people focus and to use subtleties to teach people halachic principles. Every day during *Sefirat HaOmer*, I say, "If you forgot to count last night, make sure to count at some time today." With this, we are reminding people that we are in the time between Pesach and Shavuot called *Sefirat HaOmer* and that they need to count the *Omer*. We are also teaching the halacha that if one forgot to count at night, he can get back on track by counting the next day.

Yom HaShoah, Yom HaZikaron, Yom Ha'Atzmaut, and Yom Yerushalayim

Special interviews, conversations, and recorded segments help to highlight the importance of these days. While in Israel all four of these days and their themes dominate that day's news, activities, and mood, outside of Israel one must make a special effort to connect and feel a part of them. *JM in the AM* has filled that role for all four days over many years. The appropriate music and special segments give listeners a taste of what is happening that day in the Holy Land.

Heart-Healthy Tips (17 Iyar - Lev BaOmer)

On the day that we count the 32nd day of the *Omer* — Lev BaOmer because Lev in Hebrew has the numerical value of 32 — Dr. Marc Singer, a well-known cardiologist, joins us on the air every year to share helpful information about heart health. He likes to encourage better eating habits and more regular exercise in our community in order to promote healthier hearts.

Meir Weingarten's Yahrzeit (11 Sivan)

Meir will always be missed. On his yahrzeit, we speak about the impact that he had on our audience and about the great analysis of Israel and politics that he brought to the show. He created "Meir Milim," a program segment analyzing words and phrases in the Hebrew language; the day he is missed the most is Yom Yerushalayim, when his historical presentation and analysis of the Six-Day War was one of our great annual highlights.

Interview with Rabbi Yehoshua Fass of Nefesh B'Nefesh (Thursday before Parashat Shelach)
Parashat Shelach tells the story of the Jewish people's first entrance into Eretz Yisrael. What better time to emphasize to our listeners the importance of Israel and its centrality to our religion. Rabbi Fass uses the opportunity each year to offer a *d'var Torah* on the *parsha* and discuss the necessity to remember that the future of the Jewish people is in the State of Israel.

JM in the AM 18th Anniversary Celebration

"Spoken Word Programming," Featuring Rabbi Berel Wein (The Nine Days)
During the Nine Days before Tisha B'Av, when listening to music is discouraged, we feature spoken-word programming. The centerpiece of that format are lectures by the great historian, Rabbi Berel Wein. Every year, in addition to regular interviews and conversations, we present many hours

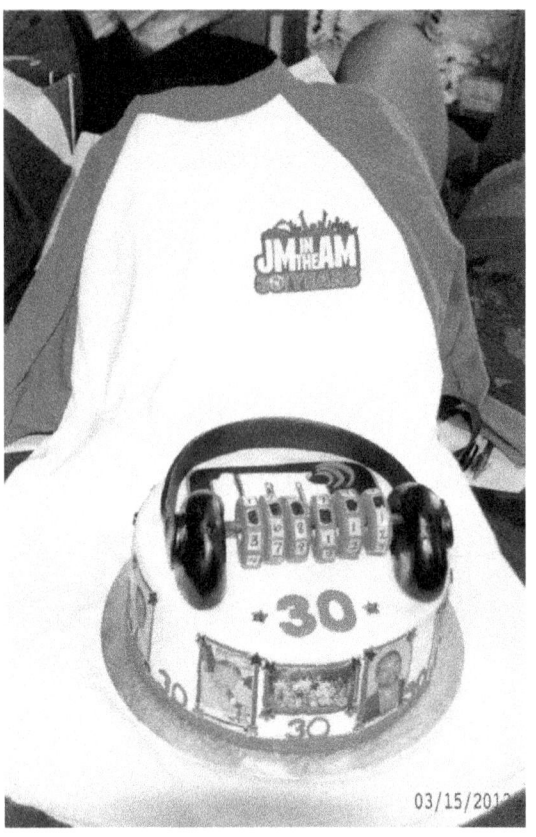
Celebrating 30 Years of JM w/ an adjustable Marathon total cake

of his appealing offerings. Listeners have told me how much they look forward to hearing his lectures. He has a unique ability to reach listeners of all backgrounds, which makes him perfect for *JM in the AM*.

Rabbi Zev Segal's Eulogy for the Lubavitcher Rebbe (3 Av)

On 3 Av in 1994, on the occasion of the *shloshim* of the Lubavitcher Rebbe, my father, Rabbi Zev Segal, delivered a moving eulogy for The Rebbe. Airing it each year gives me the opportunity to honor my father as an international audience hears how great an orator and how insightful he was.

Kinnot Service (Tisha B'Av)

For those who cannot attend *Kinnot* in shul for whatever reason, our on-air *kinnot* service provides a meaningful way to observe Tisha B'Av. I have heard from many listeners that they tune in as I read the *Kinnot* and Rabbi Goldwasser explains them. It is another innovation that developed over the years and has become a must-listen for many.

Shlomo Carlebach Stories (10 Av)

In certain years, the calendar and our customs will not allow us to return to our regular format the morning after Tisha B'Av. When that delay occurs, we bridge the gap between mourning and our regular format by playing the stories of Reb Shlomo Carlebach so that, yet again, our format hints to the fact that the day is not yet a 100% normal time.

Radio is theater of the mind and repetition and format are a very important part of our medium. We at JM in the AM have taken this philosophy seriously and have created customs and routines that have enhanced our broadcasts and our listeners' experience.

FIRE

Sunday, March 27, 2022, dawned brightly. After many months, I had finally been feeling better, following a challenging case of long Covid. We received the news that morning that my youngest child had passed his road test, a milestone that any parent can certainly appreciate. I started to feel that life post-Covid was finally taking a positive turn.

And then I got a call that my Manhattan studio was on fire.

During the time I was broadcasting every morning from the Jersey City studio, we had built a second studio on Grand Street on the Lower East Side of Manhattan as headquarters for the evening show and the 24-hour network. Over the years, the studio evolved into the epicenter of activity of the Nachum Segal Network. It was there that the full staff worked and ran shows, and after we left Jersey City in 2016, it became the exclusive home for our entire operation. It was a shrine to Jewish radio and Jewish music, housing and displaying decades of memorabilia, pictures, inscribed books, equipment, and so much more. Within minutes, the entire studio was

Lower East Side Studio Mezuzah placing by Rabbi Dovid Feinstein (FEB 2002)

engulfed in flames and everything in it was destroyed. The loss was profound, I felt as if my own home had been incinerated.

Standing outside, experiencing the trauma and devastation of this indescribable loss, I was not sure if we could ever rebound. But what was most instrumental in getting us back up and running was that there was never a moment when I felt I was going through this alone. From the very beginning, our friend and building manager, Shulie Wollman, came running from his home in Far Rockaway and, very encouragingly, informed me that we would rebuild. He was incredibly helpful in accelerating the building process.

I did not miss a morning on the air and began broadcasting remotely on Monday. Listeners were devastated, many expressing that they felt it was a

Foundation for Jewish Broadcasting co-chairs Ralph Rosenbaum and Steve Adelsberg (Lag Baomer 2021).

personal loss. While most had never seen the inside of the studio, they felt a strong connection. Yummy Schachter, whose photo with me had been displayed on a studio wall, said that he cried when he heard the news of the fire. He had to explain to his wife, who had not grown up in New York, that for those that grew up locally, it was as if part of their childhood was lost.

Many friends and colleagues came to visit and show their support. We began a fundraiser to help rebuild, and there was a tremendous outpouring of love from people who understood the importance of what we do every day.

With the help of Elie Y. Katz, we secured a temporary space in Teaneck, New Jersey and began broadcasting from there. Till today, it has proven to be both valuable and enjoyable to present the show in such a vibrant,

With Dr. Marc Singer

growing Jewish community. At the same time, we rebuilt our Manhattan home, resulting in two brand-new beautiful studios in two wonderful communities.

With the idea in my mind of multiple studios, it was only natural for me to think of a third studio in my favorite city in the world, Yerushalayim. There we have a temporary studio in the Nefesh B'Nefesh world headquarters. Three vibrant studios up and running, and an active presence in three Jewish communities is truly a silver lining of the disastrous fire.

Another significant silver lining that I will never forget is the fate of my tefillin on the morning of the fire. Every Sunday morning, I attend the six o'clock minyan. Since my recent foot surgery had prevented me from walking, I had been taking an Uber to get there. On Sundays, following minyan, I would bring my tefillin to the studio so they would be there when I needed them on Monday morning. On Sunday morning, March 27, 2022, there was a bike race in Manhattan that blocked access to my building and I could not get an Uber to take me to shul. I was forced to daven at home and so, my *tefillin* remained at home, spared from the fire.

While the pain of the fire still lingers and there is still a strong feeling of regret for all that was lost and irreplaceable, I have begun to appreciate the meaning behind the Chasidic teaching that fire brings wealth. Since the

Rabbi Yehoshua Fass visiting the brand new, rebuilt NSN Studio.

fire, we have married off two more children, had three grandchildren, and have built multiple new studios. I have a deep sense of gratitude for all that I have and I certainly appreciate it more following the loss.

Exactly a year after the fire, we hosted two large celebrations in the New York and New Jersey offices. We held an open house and invited the audience to come and see what they had helped to build. I was overwhelmed by the number of people who came to show their support. Seeing both young listeners and older listeners who have been with us since the beginning, reinforced for me that we had made the correct decision to rebuild. As I had stood at a crossroads after the fire, having to decide about how to proceed, several people suggested that perhaps it was the time in my life for me to reinvent myself and try a different path. But I remained insistent on continuing with what I had done, always tweaking and improving, but remaining faithful to the basics.

Aside from communal support, the biggest impetus for rebuilding was the constant feeling I have of being part of something meaningful. A few months before the fire, we had begun the NSN Torah of Unity project, with the hopes of writing a Sefer Torah in memory of Barry Liben *a"h*. Barry had a strong appreciation for the importance of all that NSN does for the Jewish community and he and his family were NSN's most generous donors. He was an ardent Zionist, so we decided that when the Torah was completed, we would donate it to Nefesh B'Nefesh to be part of their Aliyah Campus. Soon after the fire, I flew to Israel for the Torah dedication; I was so moved by the meaningful event that it gave me extra strength to get back on my feet and work toward recovery and rebuilding.

Throughout the many agonizing, sleepless nights following the fire and the many days that friends and family worried about the long-term effects of the trauma, it was my wife, Staci, and her endless support and patience, who eventually got me through. I was able to discover a strength I had not known that I had. It takes time to overcome grief, but with the outpouring of support, the messages of *hashgachah*, and the overflowing blessing that I have seen since the fire, I have been able to overcome adversity and emerge stronger.

EPILOGUE - ISRAEL AT WAR

As we entered the holiday of Sukkot in 2023, I was confident that my book was in its final editing stages, satisfied with the story it tells and the opinions I express in each chapter. Like most of the world, I was wholly unaware of the imminent upheaval that would reshape our lives and redefine our understanding of normalcy both in Israel and The Diaspora.. In the wake of the transformative event, the October 7th attack on Israel, it was evident that a book on Jewish communal life would be incomplete without reflecting upon the profound changes that unfolded.

On that fateful Shmini Atzeret morning, news of an Arab attack on Israel rippled through the community, first from the Rabbi's announcement in shul and then from fragments of rumors collected from various sources. With few accurate details, we were left in the dark about the extent or ramifications of the assault. Thirsty for information, I stopped at the corner store - ironically, owned by Middle Eastern immigrants - on Sunday, Simchat Torah morning and read all the daily papers.

As soon as Yom Tov ended, I felt a keen responsibility to utilize my resources to help our brothers and sisters in any way possible and to bring information from Israel to the listening audience. I hosted several political analysts and religious leaders, including commentator Ariel Kahana, Rabbi Yosef Zvi Rimon and Danny Danon, a former member of Knesset.

We featured Rabbi Ari Katz, from the Hesder Yeshiva in Sderot, who offered us a window into the situation on the Gaza border. We heard from Rabbi Doron Perez, who had one son injured on October 7th and another believed, at the time, to be held hostage in Gaza. A representative from Grilling for IDF joined us on air and encouraged Americans to donate toward their efforts to lift the spirits of those defending Israel. Rabbi Yehoshua Fass, of Nefesh B'Nefesh, provided clarity on Israel's new, dynamic landscape, giving a vivid account of the evolving realities within Israel. As the story evolved to include worldwide antisemitism, we were joined by Dov Hikind and others, who reflected on the societal, political and cultural dimensions of the changes in the world that we are all witnessing.

Two weeks after the attack I flew to Israel to broadcast from the Nefesh B'Nefesh office and from Yeshivat HaKotel in the Old City of Jerusalem. During that trip and on subsequent trips, I arrived with duffel bags representing the unwavering support of the American Jewish communities for the war effort. These bags were filled with heartfelt letters from students that expressed profound gratitude to our brave soldiers, winter coats that my wife, Staci, had diligently collected and combat helmets for the IDF. Each item symbolized our collective commitment to aiding and protecting those on the front lines.

At Yeshivat HaKotel, where my son is studying, he shared with me the profound experience of witnessing countless Israeli students depart for duty on Simchat Torah. While we were there, we were given the opportunity to interview three soldiers who, minutes before, had just returned to Yeshiva for the first time since they began serving in the war. When they walked in, I stood for them to show my deep respect for Israeli soldiers and mentioned that this was the only time I had stood for a guest on-air aside from the time my father visited the studio.

During the October trip to Israel, I visited Har Herzl, Israel's National Military Cemetery. Seeing the staggering number of new graves and the constant flow of funerals was startling and gave me a glimpse into the horrific reality that the country was experiencing. I also attended the shiva for Omar Balva, a poignant reminder of the human cost of conflict and the heavy price that our people are paying during this conflict. Omar, an American graduate of the Charles E Smith Jewish Day School who was serving in the IDF, had tragically lost his life on the Northern border.

When I returned from the short trip, I continued to host guests who could offer all perspectives on the war. I hosted community leaders from around the country whose buses to the November rally in Washington had mysteriously been canceled due to anti-semitism. We heard from Israeli vendors whose businesses had suffered due to the war and wanted American Jewish support. I interviewed people going on chesed missions to Israel and encouraged others to go. Moshe Bodner, from the Israel/IDF Chesed Fund, told of the enormous undertaking of thousands of duffels sent to Israel to help soldiers and displaced families. We featured a representative from United Hatzalah, the Beef Jerky Guys, Just One Chesed and Chessed V'Rachamim - all of whom have made significant contributions to the war effort.

In November, I embarked on my second trip to Israel, aiming to offer the audience another insightful glimpse into the country's evolving reality. I interviewed Rabbi Heshie and Rookie Billet who were running a large impromptu chesed operation. I also had the opportunity to meet with a group of doctors from New Jersey with expertise in orthopedic trauma who had volunteered their services to aid Israeli victims who had been injured in the October 7th attack. Each encounter we had proved to be truly inspiring, and our listeners deeply appreciated the unique perspective we shared.

We continued to interview people whose resilience and commitment to helping the Jewish people was both uplifting and motivating. Miriam Fuld, Ari Fuld's widow, told of her family's experiences during the war. Rabbi Avishai Milner, Rosh Yeshiva of Neveh Shmuel, told our audience of the intense pain of losing so many alumni and fathers of current students, but also of the strength and heroism that has emerged from this difficult time. A representative from Chibuk.org told of their efforts to help children who had lost loved ones in battle or terrorist attacks.

We were deeply touched by our second interview with Rabbi Doron Perez, whose heart-wrenching account of being informed that his son, Daniel, who was originally presumed captive in Gaza, had actually been tragically killed earlier, left a profound impact on us. Ellie Rothstein, of Kav Lanoar, discussed on air the state of mental health among Israelis who had experienced trauma and the arduous task ahead to deal with so many adults and children who are experiencing it.

In late December, I traveled to Israel for the third time. I interviewed many people from different segments of Israeli society including a poignant conversation with the mother of a lone soldier. A highlight of that trip was the one and a half hour interview with Jonathan Pollard who shared deep insights into the complexities of the situation in Israel while shedding light on key issues and developments.

As this long war continues, it has been inspiring to see the unwavering outpouring of support and compassion from individuals worldwide. I've seen the steadfast dedication of our audience and the broader Jewish community whose fervent commitment to praying and extending acts of kindness to those affected in Israel remains resolute despite geographical distance.

It has also been incredible to see the indomitable spirit of the Israeli people in swiftly returning to everyday life amidst the aftermath of turmoil and destruction. While normal might be a "new normal" for many, rather than succumbing to despair or dwelling on death, there's been a palpable resurgence of vitality and determination to embrace life with renewed vigor.

There has been profound change in the Israeli community. While a pervasive sense of distrust has emerged toward those entrusted with safeguarding security, there has paradoxically been a notable strengthening of bonds between different factions. Within the Charedi sector, a deep-seated sense of appreciation to the soldiers has taken root, fostering newfound solidarity and mutual respect. Simultaneously, the secular realm has experienced a resurgence of interest in observance, with a renewed curiosity regarding mitzvot such as tzitzit, lighting Shabbos candles and tefillin.

Beyond Israel, notable shifts have occurred in response to heightened antisemitic activity. These challenging circumstances have revealed our true allies amidst adversity. At the same time, the steadfast support for Israel from the global Jewish community has been striking. Individuals have demonstrated remarkable dedication and flights are full despite the exorbitant prices, showing a willingness to invest significantly or travel great distances to offer assistance or express solidarity.

On a personal level, the war and its aftermath significantly influenced many of the themes covered in this book. In the chapter on heroes I would now include the countless, incredible heroes who emerged during these trying times; individuals whose sacrifices are beyond words. The Jewish music chapter, as well, would include the many singers who have traveled to Israel to raise the spirits of soldiers and displaced families and the many songs that have been written or changed to reflect the new reality.

But, perhaps the most significant shift in this book would entail retracting my long-held, meticulously crafted opinion, which had been steadfast for many years. In Chapter 6, the chapter on Zionism, I posited that by 2008, Israel's reliance on support from the diaspora community had started to diminish. This was propelled by the combination of the ascendance of the Israeli tech sector, and the resultant economic prosperity and the economic downturn taking place at the same time in the United States. This newfound self-sufficiency reduced the need for foreign philanthropy and The Abraham Accords seemed to diminish Israel's dependence on organizations like AIPAC and government officials in the United States, bolstering its political autonomy. On October 7, the Segal theory was definitively disproved as it became apparent that Israeli society, The Knesset and the IDF still greatly depend on assistance from the diaspora Jewish community and the Washington establishment.

While I pray, along with the rest of the world, that by the time this book is published, the war will be over and the hostages and soldiers will be safe at home, the most important takeaway that I hope remains with me, and with all of us, is that Hashem is so clearly in charge, orchestrating events in ways beyond our comprehension.

It is this message that I hope reverberates throughout the book, that ultimately, everything is in Hashem's hands. While the rest of the story of my family and career remains to be told, as I reflect on the past 40 years, it becomes increasingly clear how my unique journey has underscored this truth. Hashem could take me, a kid from Newark, and place me into the most improbable situation, giving me a unique perspective and vantage point on the Jewish community and the world. I hope that I've been able to leverage my opportunities to enact meaningful change in our global community.

GLOSSARY

A"h- Stands for aleha/alav Hashalom - May s/he rest in peace

Adar, Av, Elul, Nisan - Four of the twelve Hebrew months

Amud- Lectern from which prayers are led in the synagogue

Aliyah - (lit. moving up) Moving to Israel

Ayin Hara- Evil eye

Baalei Teshuva - (lit. owners of repentance) Those who have become more observant in Judaism

Baruch Hashem - May G-d be blessed

Bimheirah B'Yameinu- It should be quickly in our days

Birkat Kohanim- The priestly blessing

Bli Ayin hara - Without an evil eye

Bris Milah- (lit. Covenant of Circumcision) - The circumcision ceremony performed on a Jewish Male, usually on the 8th day of his life

GLOSSARY

B'zchut- In the merit of

Chag Sameach- Happy Holiday

Chai- (lit. life) The numerical value of the Hebrew letters of Chai is 18

Chametz- (lit. leaven)- Food that is not eaten on Pesach (Passover)

Chareidi - (lit. one who is fearful) - Used to describe an Ultra Orthodox Jew

Chazak V'ematz- (lit. be strong and be strengthened) More power to you

Chesed- Kindness

Chizuk- Giving strength

Chol Hamoed- (lit. the regular days of the holiday)- The intermediate days of the holidays of Sukkot and Pesach

Choleh (Cholim) - Sick person/people

Chuppah- Canopy under which a Jewish wedding is performed

Derasha - A Torah lecture

Divrei Torah- Words of Torah learning

Dveykus- Deep spiritual connection to G-d

Erev - Eve of

Eruv Tavshilin- (lit. mixture of cooked foods) - A ritual that allows someone to prepare food for Shabbos on a holiday that falls out on a Friday

Esrogim- Citron fruits held on the holiday of Sukkot

Hachnasat Sefer Torah- A ceremony of bringing a new Torah scroll to a synagogue

Hallel - (lit. praise) A prayer said on special occasions

Hashgacha- Divine supervision

Kashrut- Keeping Kosher

Kedusha- Holiness

Kiddush Hashem - Sanctification of G-d's name

Klal Yisrael- The nation of Israel

Kol Hakavod- (lit. all the honor) - Well done, good job

K'siva V'chasima Tova- You should be written and sealed in the Book of Life

Lashon Hara - Speaking evil about someone

Lo Lidei Nisayon- You should not be tested

Maarat Hamachpela- The Cave of the Patriarchs in Hebron

Mamesh- Truly, really

Matzav- Situation

Mazel Tov- Good Luck

Mesirat Nefesh- (lit. giving over your soul) Sacrifice

Mi K'Amcha Yisrael- Who is like your Jewish nation

Mikvah - Ritual Bath

Mincha- Afternoon prayers

Mishnayos (Mishnayot)- a collection of teachings forming the core of the Jewish Oral Law

Mishpacha- Family

Mitzvah- Commandment, good deed

Mizrach- East

Motzai Shabbos- Saturday night

Nefesh - Soul

Neshama - Soul

Nigunim- Tunes

Parnassa- Livelihood

Parsha (Parshiyos)- Weekly Torah portion(s)

Pesach- Holiday of Passover

Pina Chama (lit. warm corner)- Roadside stands to benefit traveling soldiers

Purim- Holiday celebrating the victory of Esther and Mordechai over Haman and Amalek

Refuah Shlaimah- A complete recovery

Sefer Torah- Torah Scroll

Sefiras Haomer- The counting of the seven weeks between Pesach and Shavuot (the holiday that celebrates the giving of the Torah on Mt. Sinai)

Selichos- The prayers of asking for forgiveness for our sins said before Rosh Hashanah

Shabbos (Shabbat)- The Sabbath

Shachrit (Shachris)- Morning prayers

Shmini Atzeret/Simchat Torah- The holiday immediately following Sukkot that celebrates the completion of the Torah portions

Sheva Brachos (lit. Seven blessings) Ceremony performed at a Jewish wedding and for the week afterwards

Shofar- Ram's horn blown during the month of Elul and on Rosh Hashanah

Shul- Synagogue

Simcha- Happiness

Sukkot- Holiday of Tabernacles

Tachanun- A part of the morning and afternoon prayers

Talmid Chacham- (lit. student of wisdom) - Torah scholar

Tefillas Rabbim- Prayers of a group

Tefillin- Phylacteries- Worn by men usually during morning prayers

Tehillim- Psalms

Tisch- (lit. yiddish word for table) - Used to describe a Chasidic gathering led by the leader of a Chasidic sect

Tu B'shvat- The fifteenth day of month of Shvat- the New Year for Trees

Tzeischem L'Shalom- You should go in peace

Upsherin - (lit. Yiddish for cut off) - Ceremony in which a boy's hair is cut for the first time at the age of three.

Yarmulke - (lit. Yiddish for kippa) - Men's head covering

Yasher Koach (lit. your strength should be straight) Good job, well done

Yeshiva(t)- (lit. sitting) - School of Torah learning

Yom Haatzmaut- Israel Independence Day

Yom Hashoah - Holocaust Remembrance Day

Yom HaZikaron - Israel's Memorial Day

Yom Tov (lit. good day)- Holiday

Yom Yerushalayim- Jerusalem Day celebrating the redemption of the Old City of Jerusalem